How to Pass
The Police Officer Selection Process

2017 Edition

Copyright © 2017 CJ Benham All rights reserved

All rights reserved. Apart from any permitted use under UK Copyright Law. No part of this publication may be reproduced or transmitted in any form or by any means, electrical or mechanical, including photocopying, recording or any storage or retrieval system, without permission in writing from the publisher or under licence from the Copyright Licencing Agency Limited. Further details of such licences (for reprographic reproduction) may be obtained from the Copyright Licencing Agency Ltd, Saffron House, 6-10 Kirby Street, London EC1N 8TS

Orders: Please contact MoneyTreeMasters – via cjbenhamuk@gmail.com

First Published 2015 – Revised Edition Published January 2017 and Oct 2017

Disclaimer: Every effort has been made to ensure the accuracy of the information contained within this study guide at the time of publication. CJ Benham and any of its authors cannot be held responsible for anyone failing any part of any selection process as result of any information contained within this guide. MoneyTreeMasters and any of its team of authors cannot be held responsible for any errors or omissions within this guide, however caused. No responsibility for loss or damage occasioned by any person acting or refraining from action, as a result of the material in this publication can be accepted by MoneyTreeMasters or the author. The information within this guide does not represent the views or opinions of any third party service or organisation.

This guide is based on the teachings in our new online course that is available at

www.moneytreemasters.co.uk

Don't waste £'s or your valuable time attending an <u>expensive one day course</u>.

Sit back, relax and gain expert information, at your own pace and with the ability to review and recap all elements of the course 24/7, 365 days a year.

Contents

Preface by Author CJ Benham 11
CHAPTER 1 - PERSONAL PERFORMANCE EVALUATION 13
CHAPTER 2 – THE ROLE OF A UK POLICE OFFICER 16
CHAPTER 3 – THE UK POLICE OFFICER SELECTION PROCESS 19
CHAPTER 4 – THE POLICE OFFICER CORE COMPETENCY REQUIREMENTS 23
CHAPTER 5 – UNDERSTANDING THE STRUCTURE AND 26
FORMAT OF QUESTIONS USED BY POLICE RECRUITERS 26
Chapter 6 - Completing the Police Application Form 36
Chapter 7 – THE POLICE ONE DAY ASSESSMENT CENTRE 40
CHAPTER 8 - THE INTERACTIVE EXERCISES 43
CHAPTER 9 - THE WRITTEN TESTS 53
CHAPTER 10 – Verbal Logical Reasoning Tests 54
CHAPTER 11 – Numerical Reasoning Tests 56
CHAPTER 12 – One Day Assessment Interview 58
CHAPTER 13 – Interviews 61
CHAPTER 14 – Fitness Test 67
CHAPTER 15 – Final Thoughts 68

Introduction

Welcome to your Pass the Process study guide to Passing the UK Police Officer Selection Process. This guide is unlike any other available on the market. It has been designed to utilise specific training principles which focus on RESULTS. The results are based on selection criteria for the specific chapters "modules" that the book has been structured around.

To use this guide most effectively, try not to dip in and out of chapters, work through the guide start to finish and make use of the additional study materials available in the market.

I am sure you are more than aware of how competitive it is to become a UK Police Officer. Interestingly however, this competition is not really focused on your performance versus other candidates, it is based more on your performance against selection criteria defined by the National College of Policing.

The guide has been written in a chronological format, following the standard UK Police Officer Selection process. However, some forces are known to take slight variations from this format, in terms of selection process order of running. Please double check with the constabulary you wish to apply for.

Don't waste £'s or your valuable time attending an <u>expensive one day course</u>.

Sit back, relax and gain expert information, at your own pace and with the ability to review and recap all elements of the course 24/7

This guide is based on the teachings in our new online course

www.moneytreemasters.co.uk

The Police Officer Selection Process is not easy to complete, only 5 – 10% of initial applicants are successful on reaching the final stages. With many thousands of people applying for just a few posts, this role has always been a challenge to be recruited for.

Central to this guide is the ethos of our training techniques, these are designed to give you the edge over other candidates and our aim is to help you be successful.

Whilst it would be inappropriate for us to provide you with the exact scoring criteria the Police Service use for assessing candidates, this guide will demonstrate and provide you with Personal Performance Evaluation models to help focus your efforts in every stage of the selection process.

Thank you for purchasing this guide. I trust you will find it useful and informative. Please do leave feedback on your purchase, your views and opinions are important to me. If you want even greater insight, join the course online and set yourself apart from the competition.

Best wishes for your future.

CJ Benham

Founder – PassTheProcess & MoneyTreeMasters

Preface by Author CJ Benham

Having served both as a Special Constable and as a "Regular" Police Constable, I understand the pressures these selection processes will place upon you. In fact, being completely honest with you, it took me three attempts to become a regular officer, why? Bad luck, misfortune? Neither, the truth was that despite my abilities and what I believed I needed to demonstrate, particularly at the One Day Assessment Centre, What I thought I needed to do and what was actually required were set out of sync with each other.

Being a Police Officer is an immensely challenging, rewarding, difficult and hugely enjoyable job. No two days are the same, no two events are the same and it is this variety and the fast pace of the role that appeals to many candidates. Some of the training and experiences I gained in the role of a Police Officer, fundamentally changed me as a person, they will you to. This is a truly unique role and one that takes more personal commitment and dedication than most people would realise.

After spending several years as both a Special Constable and Police Officer, I decided that perhaps this role was not right for me, there was something more I was craving and upon reflection, I didn't really enjoy lots of paperwork (there is a huge amount in that role!). I left the force in the early 2000s and sought to expand my professional skill set in other areas.

My career has developed and grown on the foundations the Police Service instilled in me. But nothing is through chance. To me preparation has become a clear defining factor in terms of success and continual improvement. After leaving the Police Service I have held positions in both small and now global companies. The vast proportion of what I now do is in regards to Training and Performance Development. This has opened many doors for me and taken me on exciting journeys into various industries and different countries.

Back in early 2009, I was approached by an expanding provider of careers information guides and ebooks. They were looking for a tutor with a proven ability to provide the best courses for their customers. Since May 2009, I delivered ALL of their training courses which were focused on the recruitment processes for various roles. This includes amongst others, Police Officer, Firefighter, Paramedic, Train Driver, Magistrate, Army/Navy/RAF Officers. The number of people I have personally trained on these courses now reaches well in excess of 2500.

I have a firm belief that nothing should be left to chance and that true training focuses on the resulting behaviours from the delegate.

What does this mean?

Just providing information will enable some delegates to gain success, but it won't empower all to go away from a training course with strategies or reproducible techniques, that are proven to meet the requirements of the potential employer.

Please work through this guide from the very beginning to the end, despite what you may already know about the Police Selection Process. The first section of the guide is based on Personal Performance Evaluation principles, if you really want the edge over other candidates, then please take some time to reflect on how understanding these measurements are similar in principle, to the evaluation of potential Police Officers.

CHAPTER 1 - PERSONAL PERFORMANCE EVALUATION

How does someone know if they are good at performing a task or a desired set of behaviours? How does one measure the potential of a candidate, or potential employee? Is it gut feel or instinct?

This set of questions are particularly important in a number of different spheres. Training design and delivery, recruitment and continual personal/staff development all have these at the very heart of their processes.

How does this affect you in your quest to becoming a Police Officer? That is probably the most important question of all.

Personal Performance Evaluation (PPE) is a method by which given "Expert Criteria" is qualified, documented then measured against a performance provided by an individual. The concept can apply to any behavioural pattern assessment or scenario whereby skills and abilities are to be observed.

Here, let us take a complete example to demonstrate how PPE can be used.

Consider the role of a Travel Agent, working in local High St Travel Agency. Their core job function is to provide customers with quotations for holidays that meet the customers needs, sell them the holiday and any additional extras the customer may need. Whilst doing this the must follow a sales process, be polite, courteous and overcome any objections the customers may have.

The whole process would be rather onerous to document for the purpose of illustration, however, let us focus on the moment a customer walks into the Travel Agency for the first time. Below is an example of how (PPE) can be documented and measured in assessing a Travel Agent's performance.

Personal Performance Evaluation for a Sales Behaviour

Expert Criteria for Greeting Customers

How effectively did the Travel Advisor:

- **Welcome the customer to the store**: rising from their seat, using open, non-threatening body language. Correct uniform is worn and Advisor is neatly presented
- **Introduce themselves**: stating their name and asking the customer for theirs
- **Make the customer feel at ease**: without pressurising the customer, ask "What can I help you with today?"
- **Introduce relevant brochures**: through the introduction of initial qualifying questions begin to understand the customer's needs and requirements for their holiday. Select the relevant brochures based on the customer's responses.
- **Gain customer confidence and engagement**: gain commitment to taking a seat at the sales desk to further qualify and progress into the full sales presentation

Score each section on the following basis:

Rating	Description	Description of Performance
3.6 – 4.0	Expert	Performs with finesses and confidence and meets 90 percent of the criteria
3.0 – 3.5	Effective	Performs with confidence and meets 75 percent of the criteria
2.0 – 2.9	Marginal	Performs mechanically or meets 50 percent of the criteria
1.0 – 1.9	Ineffective	Performs mechanically and meets less than 50 percent of the criteria
0.0 – 0.9	Not Evident	Unable to perform any of the criteria

Notice that the Rating Scale uses a decimal numbers and this provides a range of ratings. This permits the assessor to recognise the competence of the performance whilst simultaneously identifying strengths or discrepancies in one or more of the assessed components.

What does this mean to You?

In the recruitment process for the role of a Police Officer, we are fortunate to have been given the template for "Expert Criteria" but not the "Method", or how this "Expert Criteria" should be demonstrated by the candidate. The "Expert Criteria" are more commonly known as The Police Officer Core Competencies.

Whilst having a fundamental understanding of The Police Core Competencies is essential to your successful application to the role, it is knowing how to put these into practice, in a given assessed scenario, which is the real key to success.

Personal Performance Evaluation is a time proven method of both assessing and training people and through this study guide you will learn to adopt and target your efforts to ensuring you meet "Expert Criteria" as a means to demonstrating you have got the potential to become a competent Police Officer.

Honesty and integrity are essential to your own personal evaluation of your performance, or evaluations provided by others. On our Pass The Process 1 day Police Officer Selection Course, these sessions are carried out in a safe and structured learning environment. Feedback is always given constructively and is balanced in terms of what was done well and where the delegate needs to improve on their technique and approach. There is no point telling someone they are amazing, if their performance against an agreed "Expert Criteria" is lacking. It would only serve to provide a false sense of security and wastes the delegate's valuable time.

Throughout this guide we will provide you with opportunities to carry out Personal Performance Evaluations. The principles can be applied to every stage of the recruitment process, including Application Forms, Interviews and the Police One Day Assessment.

Take the time to compare your performance against the scoring criteria, this will provide you with a solid grounding on how to prepare fully for each stage.

CHAPTER 2 - THE ROLE OF A UK POLICE OFFICER

It is extremely important that you have a full understanding of the role of a Police Officer before you begin the application process. Many people's perception of the job role is based on the influence of media and television. Unfortunately, this is slightly skewed as many aspects of a Police Officers role don't make entertaining or pleasant viewing. Rest assured there are some big highs well as big lows in this role, it's not all fast cars, foot chases and catching bad guys. There are many elements and day to day tasks which balance out the adrenaline fuelled bursts of activity.

A Police Constable is the frontline of the criminal justice system and community engagement. They will operate under general supervision, but will also be placed into scenarios where operating independently is essential. As a Police Officer you are responsible for the protection of life and property, the prevention and detection of crime and the maintenance of public order through a range of sworn powers in line with the Police Services organisational standards.

As a Constable you must be able to gather and submit information that has the potential to support law enforcement objectives. You will provide an initial response to incidents including Public Order or Road Traffic Collisions (RTCs). Through the provisions of powers given to you, your day will also include arresting, detaining or reporting individuals to Court. You will conduct priority and volume investigations which involves many differing types of techniques. As such, you will also be asked to interview victims and witnesses in relation to priority and volume investigations. Interviewing suspects in relation to priority and volume investigations is also a regular activity as you begin to build cases and investigate crime. Quite often you will search individuals and their personal property for evidence, weapons and controlled substances. Searching also includes carrying out systematic searches of vehicles, premises and open areas.

A huge part of your role is to manage conflict and being able to diffuse conflict is paramount to your success in potentially volatile situations. Police Officers also provide initial support to victims, survivors and witnesses and assess their need for further support from both the Police Service and other agencies.

Every day will present you with new challenges, different situations and unique events to deal with. Police Constables are the front line officers in the UK Police Service and nearly three quarters of all Police Officer in England and Wales hold the rank of Constable. Until very recently, all Police Officers started out in the rank of Constable before progressing up the command chain.

One you join, you will embark on a two year Probationary period in which you will be faced with differing tasks and types of training. Below is an example of a probationers schedule for the first two years of their police career.

Internal training – 10 weeks

During this period students will be taught a number of both legislative and practical skills which will give them the opportunity to develop the knowledge already learned at College or University. This includes operationally based and assessed role plays, an interview skills course and opportunities to work in the community as well as a number of lessons from experienced Police Officers in areas vital in their role as a Constable.
Please note that the training course consists of 1 week of induction followed by 10 weeks of internal training.
Normally during the 10 weeks initial training you will not be able to take annual leave.

IT Training – 2 weeks

For those new staff who have never worked within the Police in another capacity this is an opportunity to learn the computer systems that are used by the relevant constabulary and also includes a period of leave.

Tutoring Phase – 10 weeks

Once a probationary Officer's trainers are satisfied that they have adequately passed the above courses they will be released to the 'Street Duties Tutoring Unit'.
This unit has a number of experienced Tutor Constables around the County who will work with new staff to develop their skills yet further in an operational environment. Working on either a 1-1 or 1-2 basis they will deal with day to day incidents on Response teams, have an opportunity to work with local Neighbourhood teams and also to carry out interviews and low level investigations, until the tutor Constable is satisfied that the probationer is suitable for independent patrol status allowing them to work alone.

Independent Patrol Status

Once independent patrol status is achieved Students will be asked to complete a Level 3 Diploma in Policing which is designed to evidence that Probationary Officers have the skills necessary to perform at an acceptable standard as a Constable.
This period runs up to two years during which students will be supported by a PC Assessor and will have regular meetings to evidence their achievement and in order that the Assessor can identify where they need to focus their attention.

Response Strand attachment – 12 weeks

Students will first be attached to the Response strand on a Targeted Patrol Team. This will give new Constables an opportunity to work shifts with a rota developing their skills and to start toward their Diploma.

Investigation Strand attachment – 11 weeks

During an eleven week period between weeks 34 and 56 students will be given the opportunity to develop in the Investigation Strand. This will give them an opportunity to investigate crimes and carry out interviews as well as learning more about the role of a CID team.

Neighbourhood Strand attachment – 11 weeks

During an eleven week period between weeks 34 and 56 students will be given the opportunity to develop in the Neighbourhood Strand. Understanding local issues, becoming involved in community meetings and dealing with Anti Social behaviour and problems, Constables will get an insight into Neighbourhood Policing in Surrey.
During this period Probationers will also carry out a short attachment in the Tasking and Coordination Strand in order to understand their role in the force.

56 Weeks – 2 Years

At the 56 weeks stage Constables should in most cases have experienced all areas of the business and completed their Level 3 Diploma in Policing.
At this point, having given preferences to Human Resources in recent weeks and depending on the need of Strands across the Force Constables will be given their permanent posting.

2 Years – Confirmation

At the 2 year point and assuming that students have met the required standard they will be confirmed in appointment in the Office of Constable.

Congratulations, at this point you are now a fully confirmed Police Constable!

CHAPTER 3 - THE UK POLICE OFFICER SELECTION PROCESS

The selection process to becoming a UK Police Officer has a number of sections that are agreed across all counties and were issued by the College of Policing. Please be aware that you should check the order in which these elements will be staged, with the constabulary you wish to join.

Certificate in Knowledge of Policing (CKP)

This course is a relatively new phenomenon introduced in the height of the austerity measure cut backs. Essentially the course is delivered through a combination of tutor taught sessions and the completion of workbooks. Delivery is flexible and dependent on individual providers; courses are available during the week, at weekends or over evenings throughout the week. Students will be assessed at various stages through course work, the results of which will be an overall pass/fail mark.

Please be aware that this course is usually paid for by the candidate, this cost varies from provider to provider and ranges currently from £850 - £1200.

Not all constabularies require this course to be completed before joining.

Application Form

The application form is an initial test of your suitability and eligibility for the role of a Police Constable. Most of these are now completed on line and the Police Service do tend to have well written and clearly marked out application forms. Along with your basic information, Name, Address, Date of Birth etc you may be asked additional eligibility questions. Here are some example areas of eligibility:

Nationality
You must be a British or Commonwealth citizen, or an EC/European Economic Area (EEA) national, or foreign national whose stay in the UK is unrestricted.

Residency
To enable meaningful vetting, you must have been resident in the UK for the past three years.

Age
You must be aged 18 years or over to apply for the role of a police officer. There is no upper age limit, but Police Officers retire at 60.

References
The Police always take up employment references for the past three years. If you do not have three years of employment history, they will reference you via your last educational establishment.

Vetting
All applicants for employment with the Police are vetted for security reasons and for substance or alcohol abuse. All police officer applicants will be required to provide fingerprint and DNA samples by consent. A speculative search against local and national databases prior to appointment will take place and any offer of employment will be conditional upon the results meeting the required vetting standard.

Criminal Record
Police officers must respect and uphold the law. They should be law abiding and have high standards of personal behaviour and social conduct.
Applicants with criminal associations or convictions could become vulnerable to pressure to disclose information. Their position as a witness in court could also be undermined. Therefore, the Police

Service are careful about recruiting people with cautions or convictions. You must declare any caution or conviction for any criminal offence, even if this was as a juvenile or is now considered 'spent' (under the Rehabilitation of Offenders Act 1974 - Exemptions Order 1975). You must also declare any involvement with police, military or transport police investigations, even where the investigation did not lead to a prosecution.

Motoring convictions are considered with regard to the nature of the offence, the number of offences and how long ago they occurred. Candidates will be rejected if they have convictions for reckless or dangerous driving; or one offence of drink driving, drunk in charge or drugs driving within the last ten years. You must also declare other serious motoring convictions, such as driving without insurance or failing to stop after an accident or driving whilst disqualified.

Financial Status

All applicants are subject to financial vetting. An adverse credit history may jeopardise your application, although this will depend on the circumstances involved.

Business Interests

You must declare any business interests you have, so that the Police Service can judge if they are compatible with becoming a police officer.

Qualifications

A Certificate in Knowledge of Policing, endorsed by the College of Policing is required prior to a formal offer being issued by some constabularies and before an application can be made to Surrey Police. To find out more, take a look at the recruitment process. In addition all applicants must have achieved a grade C or above in GCSE English (or an equivalent qualification):

Fitness and Medical

You must be physically and mentally fit to enable you to carry out the duties required in the role of police constable and to ensure that you are able to respond to situations that may present risk to you, your colleagues or the public.

Appointment to the Police is subject to medical and physical examinations and therefore failing at the fitness stage could result in your application not being taken any further forward in the process. You must also meet our eyesight requirements as follows:

- Unaided vision should be at 6/36 with both eyes together
- Corrected vision should be 6/12 in either eye, and 6/6 with two eyes together.

Please consult your optician to ensure that you meet these requirements prior to application. The expectation is that you will provide the Opticians report for our information at the time of the medical assessment.

Driving

You must hold a full current manual driving licence before applying. Currently disqualified drivers cannot be considered.

Unsociable Hours

You must be prepared to work shifts, especially nights, on a regular basis and often including weekends and bank holidays. Consider the effect this could have on you and your family.

Diversity

You must be prepared to work with all sections of our community and to comply with the constabulary's policy on diversity.

Tattoos

You should not have tattoos that could cause offence. Tattoos are not acceptable if they are particularly prominent, garish, offensive or undermine the dignity and authority of the role of a Police Officer.

Local Initial Online Tests

Very recently some constabularies have introduced additional tests to measure your suitability to be able to complete the role of a Police Officer, these include Psychometric Tests in Spelling and Grammar, Verbal Interpretation and Numerical Fluency. Some constabularies have also included hypothetical Situational Judgement questions which are linked to the role of a Police Constable.

Initial or Telephone Interview

Some constabularies have introduced an initial force interview/telephone interview to determine the suitability of a candidate. These are usually completed ahead of attending the One Day Assessment Centre and are designed to remove candidates that do not demonstrate the correct behavioural requirements (Core Competencies) or do not demonstrate due consideration or understanding of the role of a Police Constable. Other areas potentially assessed in this part of the process is the candidates reasoning and commitment to joining the particular constabulary.

Fitness Test

The role of a Police officer is both mentally and physically demanding. As such a reasonable level of physical fitness should be maintained throughout your career and the Police will look to test this before accepting you in the role. All candidates are expected to attend and pass the fitness test, the test consists of a candidate obtaining a level 5.4 in the Bleep Test. The expectation is that you prepare yourself for the fitness test and pass it on the first attempt. However, the fitness test can be attempted on a further two occasions subject to discretion where exceptional or mitigating circumstances apply. There is no time limit for this to be completed however, you will not be able to progress any further in the recruitment process until this is successfully completed.

The Bleep Test is a controlled shuttle run between two coned off areas set at 15 meters apart. An audio CD/MP3 is played which controls the speed at which candidates are to move between the two areas. You must be in the area when the "Bleep" sounds. It starts off at a walking pace and progressively gets quicker.

One Day Assessment Centre

The Police One Day Assessment Centre is an intense event whereby candidates are required to attend by their own means.

Each section of the Assessment Centre is pass or fail and candidates can only undertake the Assessment Centre once per application. Individuals are required to achieve 50% or more to pass the National Assessment Centre however the minimum pass mark required for your application to be progressed within some constabularies can vary due to the number of high calibre candidates applying to the force. On this basis aim to score as high as you can

The assessment exercises include:
- Competency-Based Structured Interview with four questions, lasting 20 minutes in total
- a Numerical Ability Test lasting 23 minutes
- a Verbal Ability Test lasting 30 minutes
- two written exercises lasting 30 minutes each
- four interactive exercises lasting 10 minutes each

Pre-Employment Checks

During this process the Police Service will complete a number of checks on you and your background. This is for security vetting, financial and criminal convictions and references covering up to 5 years of employment if appropriate.

Medical

All candidates will be required to complete a medical and opticians questionnaire which will have to be signed off by their GP/Optician. This information will then need to be sent to the constabulary's Occupational Health team who will arrange for a candidate to attend a medical appointment and to see the Force Medical Officer in order to be signed off as FIT for service.

You will also be required to provide fingerprint, DNA samples and undergo a pre-employment substance misuse analysis by consent. A speculative search of finger prints and DNA against local and national databases prior to appointment will take place and any offer of employment will be conditional upon the results meeting the required vetting standard.

Final Interview

Although some constabularies will not require candidates to complete a Final Interview it is a widespread practice to include some form of formal interview before a final offer of employment is issued. This interview can be fairly intense and would normally involve a panel of senior serving officers and civilian staff.

CHAPTER 4 - THE POLICE OFFICER CORE COMPETENCY REQUIREMENTS

In October 2013 the National Policing Improvements Agency (now defunct and replaced by the College of Policing) released six new Police Officer Core Competency requirements. These are key skills and abilities that have been determined as to what makes a good Police Officer. The six Core Competencies are:

Serving the Public

Openness to Change

Service Delivery

Professionalism

Decision Making

Working with Others

If you are going to increase your chances of success in the selection process, then having a full understanding of these and what they mean to potential candidates is essential.

Below is the full description of each Core Competency:

Serving the public
- Demonstrates a real belief in public service, focusing on what matters to the public and will best serve their interests.
- Understands the expectations, changing needs and concerns of different communities, and strives to address them.
- Builds public confidence by talking with people in local communities to explore their viewpoints and break down barriers between them and the police.
- Understands the impact and benefits of policing for different communities, and identifies the best way to deliver services to them.
- Works in partnership with other agencies to deliver the best possible overall service to the public.

Serving the public is all about, great customer service but also being able to approach all members of the community and being able to build bridges and reach out to them. Here the Police Service are looking for you to be able to demonstrate how well you are able to look after people, give great customer focus and be willing to engage with the whole community.

Openness to change
- Positive about change, adapting rapidly to different ways of working and putting effort into making them work.
- Flexible and open to alternative approaches to solving problems.
- Finds better, more cost-effective ways to do things, making suggestions for change and putting forward ideas for improvement.
- Takes an innovative and creative approach to solving problems.

Openness to change is a completely new direction for the Police Service. Today's modern Police Service is still largely inefficient and is going to need to adapt as time goes by. What the Police

Service are looking to establish with this Core Competency, is that you are the type of candidate who will be flexible in your approach to situations, adapt and be positive about organisational change and be willing to work through those changes, being loyal and committed to the cause.

Service delivery
- Understands the organisation's objectives and priorities, and how own work fits into these.
- Plans and organises tasks effectively, taking a structured and methodical approach to achieving outcomes.
- Manages multiple tasks effectively by thinking things through in advance, prioritising and managing time well.
- Focuses on the outcomes to be achieved, working quickly and accurately and seeking guidance when appropriate.

Service delivery is focusing on you delivering the best value for money whilst completing your role as a Police Officer. The Police Service is paid for by the community, as such, we want the best possible service for our investment. This relates to the phrase of "proactive policing" whereby you will not be the type of person to arrive on duty to "see what happens". Here they are looking for you to demonstrate how you take a structured and methodical approach to your work to gain the best return.

Professionalism
- Acts with integrity, in line with the values and ethical standards of the Police Service.
- Takes ownership for resolving problems, demonstrating courage and resilience in dealing with difficult and potentially volatile situations.
- Acts on own initiative to address issues, showing a strong work ethic and demonstrating extra effort when required.
- Upholds professional standards, acting honestly and ethically, and challenges unprofessional conduct or discriminatory behaviour.
- Asks for and acts on feedback, learning from experience and developing own professional skills and knowledge.
- Remains calm and professional under pressure, defusing conflict and being prepared to step forward and take control when required.

Professionalism is a challenging competency. This is mainly on the basis that in a true competency frame working programme, the description applied to this would not be acceptable. There is quite simply far to many aspects and "competencies" to roll into one given scenario to achieve the overall description of "Professionalism". Not only are the Police Service looking for you to demonstrate courage, resilience and being able to act on your own initiative, they are looking for your honesty, integrity and you respect for race and diversity. You must be able to challenge unprofessional or discriminatory behaviour as well as asking for feedback and learning from this. Finally the ability to defuse volatile situations and take personal responsibility for the situation are also included in this Core Competency.

Decision making
- Gathers, verifies and assesses all appropriate and available information to gain an accurate understanding of situations.
- Considers a range of possible options before making clear, timely, justifiable decisions.
- Reviews decisions in the light of new information and changing circumstances.
- Balances risks, costs and benefits, thinking about the wider impact of decisions.
- Exercises discretion and applies professional judgement, ensuring actions and decisions are proportionate and in the public interest.

In direct paradox to Professionalism, Decision Making is a very clearly and well defined description of a key skill all good Police Officers retain. A vast proportion of your role as a Police Constable is based on your ability to make quick and timely decisions based on justification and your discretionary powers.

Working with others
- Works co-operatively with others to get things done, willingly giving help and support to colleagues.
- Is approachable, developing positive working relationships.
- Explains things well, focusing on the key points and talking to people using language they understand.
- Listens carefully and asks questions to clarify understanding, expressing own views positively and constructively.
- Persuades people by stressing the benefits of a particular approach, keeps them informed of progress and manages their expectations.
- Is courteous, polite and considerate, showing empathy and compassion.
- Deals with people as individuals and addresses their specific needs and concerns.
- Treats people with respect and dignity, dealing with them fairly and without prejudice regardless of their background or circumstances.

Don't be drawn into the title of this particular Core Competency. Whilst working with others would normally translate to Team Work, there is far more to this competency, including your ability to communicate effectively with others, persuasion skills and the ability to treat all people with respect and dignity. Again this relates to an absolute requirement for all Police Officers to have respect for race and diversity.

CHAPTER 5 – UNDERSTANDING THE STRUCTURE AND FORMAT OF QUESTIONS USED BY POLICE RECRUITERS

There are a number of differing questions and styles of questions that can be applied in a recruitment process. All have positive and negative effects for both the interviewer and the delegate. In this guide we are going to focus on the three major types of question that can be asked both on an Application Form and in Interviews.

We have included this section in the guide as a means to enable you to prepare fully for each stage of the process, understand what is being asked of you and to empower you with the best methods to tackle these types of questions.

"Knowledge is power"

– Sir Francis Bacon, English Philosopher

"Victorious warriors win first and then go to war, while defeated warriors go to war first and then seek to win"
— Sun Tzu, *The Art of War*

General Questions
General questions are a nuisance in an interview environment. Firstly from the point of view of a candidate, the wide reaching nature of the question lacks direction, causes confusion and does not provide the opportunity to be really focused on what the interviewer is looking for. The plus side is that is enables the candidate to really express themselves and sell why they meet the job requirements.

From an interviewers perspective these types of questions are flawed. By its' nature the question can lead the candidate to talk about completely irrelevant subject matter and or waffle. Also, despite what the candidate states, it is more a case of them telling the interviewer rather than the interviewer seeing PROOF that the candidate is ideal for the job. The interview is able to see if the candidate can think fast on their feet and communicate well. However, these questions are traditionally considered as non-evidential.

Example: "So, tell us a bit you yourself"

Motivational Questions
These questions are flawed similarly to General Questions in that they are still wide reaching and both interviewer and candidate can suffer the same pitfalls from the questioning style. The variation from General Question is that these types of question will always have a "Why?" about them.

Candidate can provide a number of very honourable and worthy responses to this type of question, however too often these tend to be clichéd and rather generic.

The interviewer will therefore have to try to stave of boredom and repetitiveness, particularly if they are interviewing a number of people on the same day. These are also considered as non-evidential questions

Example: "Why do you want to become a Police Officer?"

Competency Based Questions

Competency based question are very different to Motivational or General questions. This type of questioning technique has been designed to enable the interviewer to theoretically observe a candidates behavioural pattern when dealing with a past event or scenario. The thought process being that should a candidate be able to cope with a situation in the past, then the likelihood is that they would be able to cope with a similar situation again in the future.

For the candidate, this type of question should be relatively easy. It is predictable and guaranteed that you will be asked questions in this format, as such, preparation should be easy. The challenges with this type of question is that 1) the candidate didn't prepare and therefore has no example to discuss and 2) the example or scenario discussed with the candidate does not match the competency being assessed by the interviewer.

Example: "Please provide an example of where you have challenged someone's behaviour that was perhaps inappropriate or discriminatory"

Because these questions have a structured format for asking them, there is also a structure way to answer them. This is called the STAR technique. Follow this format and you are long way to being successful in the interview when asked this type of question. More on this later in this chapter.

The Police Service are masters of the competency based question and you will face this particular type of questioning at various stages of the selection process.

Application Forms traditionally contain a competency based section, which is pass or fail

One Day Assessment Centre Interview is limited to four questions and these are all competency based.

Initial and Telephone Interviews would almost certainly contain some competency based questions

Final Interviews are also known to have them included.

Question Style Identification Exercise

Take a look at the below 10 example questions and note down which type of question you think it is, General, Motivational or Competency Based?

1. "Give us an overview of your career"
2. "Give me an example of when you have worked as part of a team to achieve a difficult task"
3. "Tell me about a time when you made a mistake, what you did to correct it and how you learnt from that experience"
4. "Why do you want to join this particular company?"
5. "What is your biggest achievement to date in your personal life?"
6. "Please tell us why you would be suitable for this job and what skills you believe you can bring to the role?"
7. "Describe a time when you have had to take the lead in a challenging situation"
8. "Why do you want to become a Police Officer?"
9. "What motivates you to go to work every day?"
10. "Take me through your career progression over the last 5 years"

Understanding the style or type of question you are being posed is half of the battle when it comes to providing a potential employer with what they are looking for. Once the recognition of these differing questions becomes second nature to you, you will have a greater ability to focus your response appropriately and score highly in this assessment area.

Tactics for Dealing with General Questions

These questions can be viewed both negatively and positively from a candidate's perspective. The free ranging openness can give you plenty of opportunity to ensure your assessor has ample opportunity to see that you have the right qualities to become a Police Officer. However, if you are supplied with a General question in an interview, do try to direct it back to the interviewer to gain a more structured question.

A successful phrase to use to enable you to do this could;

"There is a great deal I could tell you about me, I could talk about my work and career or my home and family life, where would you prefer me to start?"

By asking an interviewer this question you are seeking to narrow down the question in a non-confrontational manner. However, the interviewer responds, you will now have a more defined structure to follow. Make sure anything you mention, whether work or pleasure related, the skills and abilities you mention must match the role of a Police Officer. Make sure you use lots of keywords and phrases from the descriptions of the Core Competencies.

Tactics for Dealing with Competency Based Questions

Because these are structured questions there is a structured method for answering them. Make sure you learn and adopt this format for responding to Competency Based Questions.

The importance of this is so high that, without a thorough understanding of the Core Competencies, you will not pass the process, without a thorough understanding of this technique, you will not pass the process. Make sure you are completely comfortable and happy with this method of responding to questions.

S ituation - set the scene as you are telling a story. Give the setting. "Whilst working in my role as a cashier at a local supermarket

T ask – why you were there and what was the issue that was developing? "It was my role to ensure all customers were happy and felt they were being looked after. One customer had a problem with…..

A ctions – talk about what you did and what you said. Be sure to use lots of "I" statements. "I noticed, I suggested, I intervened"

R esults – what happened at the end due to your actions. Be sure to have a positive outcome. You are after all, telling a story and everyone likes a happy ending

Be sure to base your answers on real events that you have experienced. This will help you to write in greater detail. Try also to use examples of situations you felt were challenging and difficult. This will also enable you to respond with more depth and emotional content. To score higher and ensure your success, use keywords and phrases from the Police Officer Core Competencies. This will assist the assessors in noticing you are fluent with the job role and makes it easier for them to recognise what you are trying to say and how your experience fits with the role of a Police Constable.

Tactics for Dealing with Motivational Questions

At some stage in the process to becoming a Police Officer you will be asked "Why do you want to become a Police Officer?" This is almost a certainty. Having worked with, trained and coached hundreds of people over the last 10 years, I can normally predict the content and style of response given to this question by the vast proportion of potential candidates. It will have words to the effect of:

"I want to become a Police Officer because I want and interesting and rewarding career which is challenging and different every day. I would love to have the opportunity to progress and develop in the future and would be proud to be given the chance to give something back to the community."

And or may include:

"I'm a real people's person, so I don't want a job that is constrained by a desk, I want to be active and placed into different scenarios every day where I can make a difference."

Or

"It's been an ambition of mine to become a Police Officer for x years (or from childhood). It's something I've always wanted to do and appreciate it's a vocation, not just a job"

Is there anything fundamentally wrong with these responses? No and probably reading this book, something may seem familiar in the above. However, let's analyse these responses and look at them from the other side of the interview table, from the Interviewer's perspective.

"I want to become a Police Officer because I want and interesting and rewarding career which is challenging and different every day. I would love to have the opportunity to progress and develop in the future and would be proud to be given the chance to give something back to the community."

Says to the interviewer –

"I don't want to be bored at work because I need to be stimulated constantly meaning, I'm probably high maintenance as an employee. Whilst constantly demanding your attention, I want to climb the hierarchal ladder for more money and I want to do this in a job that makes me feel good about myself"

"I'm a real people's person, so I don't want a job that is constrained by a desk, I want to be active and placed into different scenarios every day where I can make a difference."

Says to the interviewer –

"I like to hang around with people in groups, so I am probably not much use out on my own. I would rather be out and active than being under your watchful eye. I also want to be challenged everyday so that I can feel good about myself"

"It's been an ambition of mine to become a Police Officer for x years (or from childhood). It's something I've always wanted to do and appreciate it's a vocation, not just a job"

Says to the interviewer –

"I've been brought up watching Cops and Interceptors and I think policing is about fast cars, chasing bad guys and I'm up for some adrenalin hits"

I have been rather blunt and facetious in the interview thoughts, but this has been to try to highlight some common pitfalls candidates fall foul of when answering this incredibly important question. When reviewing those initial responses again, I am sure you will see that there are a number of hugely clichéd answers, which become tiresome and boring to the interviewer. More importantly the responses are hugely SELFISH. Everything mentioned benefits the candidate, not the Police Service.

What would the Police Service prefer to hear?

Below is a technique that I have previously been very reluctant to share with people, not because it is unethical and not because it is cheating. I've held this back because this method for answering the big motivational question of "Why do you want *this* job" has, since I finalised it's structure in 2013, been *so* successful for me and those few I have shared it with, that I wanted to keep it for myself. I didn't want MY competition at interview stage having anywhere near as good a tactic as this. But as I said at the start of this book, I'm going to give you the best tactics I know to help you achieve your goal in becoming a Police Officer.

This technique is designed to be greatly different from any other candidate response. Whilst I do not wish to provide you with a script, there are key phrases and nuances in tone and speech pattern that are particularly important in how this is delivered in an Interview. Please note, the terminology will be slightly different, but there is no reason why this same structure cannot be used on the Application Form, if you are asked. "Why do you want to become a Police Officer?"

Employers have a number of major concerns when hiring people and the Police Service are no different. Remember, recruiting people is incredibly expensive business, so they want to make sure they get it right. Among other important considerations they will have:

1. Is this the right person for the job? Do they have the right skills and potential to do well? Do they have evidential proof they have the Police Officer Core Competencies
2. Will they fit into our organisational culture or cause issues?
3. Will they enjoy working here, be committed to our training programme and ultimately provide a return on our investment in recruiting them?

These are fairly standard factors for any recruitment process and the Police Service is no different. The best response to that major question of "Why do you want to become a Police Officer?" Will provide the recruiters with total comfort and certainty that you answer YES to all of those points above.

Before you can begin to answer this question using this strategy, there are key areas of research that you must complete.

1. Research the constabulary you wish to join. Gain a thorough understanding of the county/counties they operate in, the local demographics, review and understand their website, in particular their ABOUT US page. On this page there will be key information in regards to the culture and ethos that constabulary are trying to foster in their organisation.
2. Your own experiences in relation to the Police Officer Core Competencies. This may seem daft, but a great deal of us live in our tiny bubbles and go about our daily lives without realising what we actually do. Naturally big events or unusual things tend to stick in our memories, but rest assured, you will demonstrate elements of the Police Officer Core Competencies on a daily basis. The trick is to find them and use them.

Come back to the guide once you have completed this exercise.

Here is the structure broken down into sections:

Section 1 – Employer Organisation Understanding and Values Alignment
Section 2 – Understanding the Role and Evidence of Skill Set
Section 3 – Flippancy and Concentration Recovery
Section 4 – Close the Conversation

Answering the question
The opening sentence to this response is very important, mainly because if you start with the traditional "I want to become a Police Officer because…." It will lead down the path of every other candidate. As such, try to open with a statement which keeps you well away from that line of response. Below is a structure, with phrases and terminology that have proven to be very successful and have drawn the right responses from many different interview panels.

Why do you want to become a Police Officer?

Section 1 – Aligning Yourself with the Organisation's Values
"Firstly, please let me tell you why I want to join this constabulary. I have spent a great deal of time researching your organisation and I can see it has an excellent reputation for………"**(insert the elements of research about the organisation)**

"These are the kind of values and ethics that resonate with the type of person that I am. It's because of this that I believe that I would fit in well in this constabulary."

Section 2 – Understanding the Role and Evidencing the Skill Set
"I have also completed an intensive amount of research on the role of a Police Officer and I know that a good Police Officer needs to have certain skills and abilities like…XYZ……….**(insert 3 of the Core Competencies)**"

This is where you will take a tactical change in response type, moving away from Motivational to Competency Based. This is because Competency Based responses provide more evidence. You must ensure that the 3 Core Competencies you mentioned before are evidence in the scenario you provide.

"During my time working as a……."

S

T

A

R"

Now you will want to re –emphasise the 3 Core Competencies you mentioned earlier.

"So I know I have the abilities of XYZ)

Repeat the process by teeing up more Core Competencies.

"I also know that a good Police Officer needs to have the abilities of ……ABC. Whilst in my role as a….

S

T

A

R

So I know I also have the skills of ABC"

At this point you will now need to bring the assessor back on track. They will have been initially intrigued and impressed with hearing something new and different. Having used this structure a number of times, especially in interviews, this is a point where I have seen interviewers begin to start questioning where the response is going. The will like it, but they were expecting the standard response style they will get from every other candidate. You will need to provide this to them, but in a fashion that is not detrimental to all the good work you have already completed.

Section 3 – Flippancy and Interviewer Concentration Recovery
This has to be delivered in an interview in a very off hand, throw away manner. What you are trying to do is compartmentalise the standard motivational style response and make it as tiny an aspect of your motivation to join the Police as possible.

"Like everyone else applying for this role, of course I want an interesting and rewarding career that is challenging and varied every day. And yes, I do want to give something back to the community but I am sure you hear that from all the other candidates and it is rather clichéd."

Section 4 – Close the Conversation
This is where you need to be absolutely focused and ensure the assessor or interviewer is able to recognise that it is this point where they need to take stock of your response and make a decision. This is achieved by placing what we call in sales techniques a "Close" at the end. This "Close" is very subtle, you are not saying "So are you going to give me the job" but the phrasing enables the assessor/interviewer to make that leap on their own.

"But, the main reason that I want to become a Police officer is because…."

You must be absolutely crystal clear and extremely careful in what you say next. Too many people in interviews feel the need to provide grandiose and flamboyant reasons for wanting a job or provide opportunity for the interviewer/assessor to pull the reasoning apart.

Don't let this happen to you!

Tell the whole and pure truth! Direct from the fundamental reason why you are wanting to become a Police Officer rather than any other job out there. Why a Police Officer and not a plumber or a receptionist?

Because you think you can do it!

Here though, terminology is really important. Don't say *"I think I can do it"* because this demonstrates uncertainty. Don't say *"I feel I can do it"* because again the interview may "feel" you can't. Finally don't say *"I know I can do it"* because this can be construed as arrogant.

*"The main reason that I want to become a Police Officer is because, I **believe** I have the right skills and the right qualities to go on to become a competent, safe and successful Police Officer"*

Here is the closing phrase that must be added to the end of the structure. It's very small, but very powerful.

"and that is why I am here." On an Application Form you must state instead *"and that is why I am applying for this position"*

I would encourage you to use the phrase "I believe" as it is very powerful, particularly when delivered with total conviction. Also, in today's modern society people don't like to challenge others beliefs.

Here is the structure displayed in full format. Try to use your own language and phrasing, this is not a script, but I would encourage you to follow the structure.

Why do you want to become a Police Officer?

Firstly, please let me tell you why I want to join this constabulary. I have spent a great deal of time researching your organisation and I can see it has an excellent reputation for valuing a diverse workforce, honesty and accountability. As a public service, you aim to keep the public safe, be there when they need you and are relentless in your approach to pursuing criminals. These are the kind of values and ethics that resonate with the type of person that I am. It's because of these similarities, that I believe that I would fit in well in this constabulary.

I have also completed an intensive amount of research on the role of a Police Officer and I know that a good Police Officer needs to have certain skills and abilities like being open to change, professional and being able to build good working relationships.

During my time working as a tutor for a training consultancy, I was faced with a particularly challenging incident where one of my employees was not preparing course materials or researching their programme subject matter. I was my role to ensure that delegate attending training courses all received the best level of service possible. This was not happening due to my colleagues' apparent lack of enthusiasm towards his role. I approached him in a confident but non-threatening manner to establish what his concerns and potential issues were. Because I demonstrated to him that I would treat our conversation in a fair and appropriate manner, he felt at ease to divulge some family issues he was facing. As such, and treating the nature of the matter with utmost integrity, I was able to adapt his preparation programme and adopt a new way of getting information to the training team. He felt happy that I had demonstrated that he was valued both as a team member and as an employee, so felt happier in his role and was better able to cope.

Because the situation had a positive outcome, I know that I have the ability to work well with others, be open to changes in the work place and remain professional at all times.

I also know that a good Police Officer needs to have other abilities like having a genuine focus on public service, delivering high standards in their work and being decisive in their actions.

Whilst travelling home from an event last year I was in the middle lane of the motorway when I was overtaken by a 4x4 Pickup. The vehicle proceeded to ram a car about 150 yards in front of me, causing it to spin and crash into the central reservation before rolling back into the carriageway in front of me. I reacted quickly and calmly, stopping at a safe distance from the vehicle and ensured the traffic behind me had also come to a safe stop. I then approached the crashed car and assisted two ladies from the vehicle to the hard shoulder. I had to get them out of the stricken vehicle as it was in an unsafe position and leaking fuel. I made sure they were both okay despite the shock of the incident. I then returned to my vehicle and called the emergency services who arrived shortly after. Because I took decisive action, the two ladies were protected from further injury and no other road users were caught up in the incident. I felt it was my duty to assist these two ladies in their time of need and I stayed in contact with them following the incident. Several months after I received a letter of thanks which was sent to my managing director.

I know therefore that I am decisive have a genuine interest in helping the public and can work to high standards even in stressful situations.

Like everyone else applying for this role, of course I want an interesting and rewarding career that is challenging and varied every day. And yes, I do want to give something back to the community but I am sure you hear that from all the other candidates and it is rather clichéd.

The main reason that I want to become a Police Officer is because, I believe I have the right skills and the right qualities to go on to become a competent, safe and successful Police Officer and that is why I am here.

Naturally this same tactic can be used on the Application Form. Just replace the some of the phrasing in the flippant section and in the close.

Have a go at constructing your own version of this format. Input your own scenarios for the evidential section and practice the delivery of this structure. The more you use it, the easier it becomes and the more natural it sounds. The more natural it sounds, particularly in an interview, the more convincing you are to the panel.

Chapter 6 - Completing the Police Application Form

It is imperative that you submit a strong application form if you want to become a Police Officer. A professional application form which meets the selection criteria will ensure that you have an advantage over the other applicants. When there are thousands applying, this is critically important. Remember, if your application is unsuccessful at any point of the police recruitment process, it will be six months before you will be able to apply again, so let's try to ensure your success at the very first attempt.

There are four major sections to the Police Application Form.

1. Personal Information
2. Employment History
3. Education and Qualifications
4. Competency Based Questions – usually 10 questions

To ensure all applications are marked fairly and without prejudice, the assessing recruitment staff only receive certain sections of your application form. This means that your personal information is removed from the assessment process. This includes all of the Equal Opportunities Monitoring information. As long as you are eligible to apply, none of this data will have a direct impact on your application.

The assessing staff will focus in on the Competency Based Questions section of the application form. This is pass or fail section. As such you must ensure you provide the best answers possible. You will need to put in extra effort to demonstrate you have the right skills to match the competencies that are being assessed.

Marking follows the below format and the scoring is matched to the average scores of all candidates.

- An A-grade means that when compared to other candidates, your score was within the top 15%
- A D-grade answer means that your answers were in the bottom 15% when compared to other candidates
- Your marks are added up to give an overall score. To pass, candidates must achieve a 'B' grade in 3 out of the 4 competencies, or a 'B' grade in 2 out of the 4 competencies, as well as a 'B' grade overall

Force Recruitment Webpages

England

Avon & Somerset Constabulary
Bedfordshire Police
Cambridgeshire Constabulary
Cheshire Constabulary
City of London Police
Cleveland Police
Cumbria Constabulary
Derbyshire Constabulary
Devon & Cornwall Police

Dorset Police
Durham Constabulary
Essex Police
Gloucestershire Constabulary
Greater Manchester Police
Hampshire Constabulary
Hertfordshire Constabulary
Humberside Police
Kent Police
Lancashire Constabulary
Leicestershire Police
Lincolnchire Police
Merseyside Police
Metropolitan Police Service
Norfolk Constabulary
North Yorkshire Police
Northamptonshire Police
Northumbria Police
Nottinghamshire Police
South Yorkshire Police
Staffordshire Police
Suffolk Constabulary
Surrey Police
Sussex Police
Thames Valley Police
Warwickshire Police
West Mercia Police
West Midlands Police
West Yorkshire Police
Wiltshire Police

Wales

Dyfed-Powys Police
Gwent Police
North Wales Police
South Wales Police

Scotland

Police Scotland

Northern Ireland

Police Service of Northern Ireland

Non-Home Office Forces
British Transport Police
Civil Nuclear Constabulary
Ministry of Defence Police
Port of Dover Police
National Crime Agency

The Competency Based Questions

These are all focused on the Core Competencies as mentioned previously. Ensure you read each question very carefully and match your examples to the competency being assessed. Try to ensure that you are providing clear and focused key words from the Core Competency document, so that it is easier for your application form assessor to recognise you are the right candidate. Usually the questions are worded in a format that has the "Headline" question followed by a series of "prompts". You will need to apply the STAR technique in order to meet the required standard for a successful answer.

Top 10 Tips for a Successful Application form

1. Complete the form and submit it as quickly as possible – Don't wait for the last day of submission
2. Check spelling, punctuation and grammar are all correct
3. Don't lie about any of your experiences
4. Read all of the instructions and follow them precisely
5. Don't rely on standard postage if submitting a paper document, send it recorded
6. Try to use examples of scenarios that you found challenging or difficult, you will naturally write in greater depth and with more emotion
7. Ensure you pack plenty of key words and phrases from the Core Competencies into your answers
8. Keep a copy of everything, you may want to refer to it at a later stage in the selection process.
9. Never ever lie about a scenario you have faced
10. If you are asked about working with others or team working scenarios, still use "I" statements. People tend to revert to "We" and the focus will be drawn away from you.

Before proceeding to the next stage of this book, you should complete some practice questions and evaluate your performance against the Personal Performance Evaluation for each one. Be truthful in your self-analysis as scoring yourself too highly or too harshly will only achieve delusion or demotivation respectively.

Here are some practice questions to consider.

1. Please provide an example of where you have challenged someone's behaviour that was perhaps discriminatory or inappropriate.
2. Tell me about a time when you have worked with a group of others to achieve a difficult task.
3. Give me an example of where you have gone above and beyond your normal working requirements.

4. Please tell us about a time when you have had to adapt to a new way of working and its impact on you.
5. Please provide an example of when you have delivered excellent customer service.
6. Give an example of when you have had to make a decision that perhaps others disagreed with.

Chapter 7 – THE POLICE ONE DAY ASSESSMENT CENTRE

Before attending the Police One Day Assessment Centre, you will be sent an information pack which outlines a tremendous amount of important information. This chapter will provide an in-depth overview of the information so that you can begin to prepare well in advance.

The Police Recruitment 1 Day Assessment Centre will last for approximately 5 hours and you may not have opportunity to stop for a break within this time frame. As such, ensure you have something to eat and drink before you arrive. The assessment centre consists of the following key elements:

- Interactive exercises (Role Plays)
- A competency based structured interview
- Psychometric tests

All candidates must also be able to demonstrate an acceptable level of competence in written communication. The constabularies have a number of options in how they assess written communication as outlined below:

1. Complete two written exercises completed **before** the assessment centre – candidates would need to pass the written exercises to attend the Police Recruitment 1 Day Assessment Centre.
2. Complete two written exercises **during** the assessment centre – candidates would need to pass this written exercises in order to be successful at the assessment centre.
3. Accept a qualification of written English **before** the assessment centre – forces may ask candidates to complete a specific qualification, or provide evidence of having completed a specific qualification before they are able to attend the Police Recruitment 1 Day Assessment Centre. The qualification can be at the constabulary's discretion, but must be at a minimum level of Functional Skills Level 2 English (or equivalent).
4. Accept a qualification of written English obtained **after** the assessment centre – constabularies may ask candidates to complete or provide evidence of having completed a specific qualification after they have attended the assessment centre. Candidates must have completed the qualification prior to being signed off as a Police Constable.

Currently, the vast majority of constabularies will choose option 2 and will assess you at the Police Recruitment 1 Day Assessment.

Everyone who attends the assessment centre will complete the same tests and scenarios. This is to ensure fairness and equality for all candidates on the day.

How are you assessed?

You will be assessed on **what** you do and **how** you do it. Trained assessors measure how you perform in each of the exercises which relate to specific core competencies. They then use information from all of the exercises to determine whether or not you have met the national standard by how well you demonstrated evidence across the competency areas being assessed.

The trained assessors assess competencies which are particularly relevant to the role of a Police Constable. In addition, they will assess oral communication across the interactive and interview exercises and written skills in the written exercises, as these are also relevant for the role of a Police Constable.

Role Plays

In the role plays you are to assume the role of a newly appointed Customer Services Officer at the fictitious retail and leisure complex called "The Westshire ® Centre". Naturally this place does not exist and it's concept has been created solely for the purposes of the assessment centre.

In addition to the Information for Candidates pack sent to you in advance of attending the assessment centre, you will be provided with The Westshire ® Centre Welcome Pack. Enclosed is an overview of your main duties and responsibilities as a "Customer Services Officer" along with details about The Westshire ® Centre and its policies in regards to Equality and a Code of Conduct.

There are four Interactive Exercises to complete. Each is 10 minutes long but this is split into two segments. Firstly the Preparation Phase, which will last for 5 minutes. Here you will be provided with a brief to read and given opportunity to make notes and plan how to handle the roleplay. The second phase is the Activity Phase. This will also last for 5 minutes and it is in this section where you will enter a room and meet the role play actor. More on this in the Role Play Chapter!

Competency Based Structured Interview

The Competency Based Structured Interview has changed as of August 2015. It will last for 20 minutes in total with you being asked 4 specific questions. 2 questions will be competency based, specifically asking you to provide evidence on how you have handled situations in your past and how you reacted to them. Here is where you use the STAR model, as discussed in Chapter 5.

The other 2 questions will be about your motivations and values and how these relate to the Police Service.

You will have up to 5 minutes to answer each question, if you go over the time allowed, you will be stopped by the interviewer. The interviewer may also ask further probing questions to try to extract a fuller response from you.

This new interview structure now assesses all 6 Core Competencies along with your Oral Communication abilities.

More on this in the Competency Based Structured Interview Chapter.

Psychometric Tests

You will be subject to 2 types of test in this section of the One Day Assessment Centre. Numerical Reasoning and Verbal Logical Reasoning. All tests will be conducted in an exercise room, under exam style conditions with other candidates in your group.

The Numerical Reasoning test changed in 2014 to now include the use of a calculator, which will be provided for you at the assessment centre (don't take your own!). For this test you will need to be able to answer multiple choice questions. This will measure your ability to use numbers in a rational way, correctly identifying logical relationships between numbers and drawing conclusions and inference from them.

The Verbal Logical Reasoning test measures your ability to make sense of a situation when you are given specific written information about it. The test is split into two sections – Section A and Section

B. Section A of this test has **three** possible answers where only ONE of which is correct, whereas Section B has **four** possible answers of which only ONE is correct.

In **Section A** they will give you a number of conclusions which you might come to. You must look at each conclusion and work out if:

A the conclusion is **true** given the situation described and the facts known about it;

B the conclusion is **false** given the situation described and the facts known about it; or

C it is **impossible to say** whether the conclusion is true or false given the situation described and the facts known about it.

In **Section B** they will give you four statements and you will be required to evaluate which ONE of the **four** statements is the best answer, given the information provided.

Once you have made your decision you will then fill in the appropriate space on an answer sheet provided.

More on this in the Psychometric Tests Chapter

Written Test

Regardless of whether the written tests are completed before or during the assessment centre, all candidates will complete two written exercises. Both exercises will last for circa 30 minutes. You will be shown into an exercise room along with the other candidates in your group. You will then be provided with a thorough briefing before you start each exercise. Paper and pens will be provided, together with documents to write your response. You may make rough notes on a separate piece of paper, which will not be assessed.

The written skills being tested at the assessment centre are your ability to comprehend and summarise information accurately, structure responses logically and to use spelling and grammar correctly.

More on this in the Written Test Chapter

CHAPTER 8 - THE INTERACTIVE EXERCISES

For the vast proportion of candidates, the role play section of the one day assessment centre is probably one of the most daunting tasks. Certainly from the feedback I have received over the last seven years of delivering training on how to pass this process, candidates lose the greatest amount of confidence when preparing for the interactive exercises. In this chapter, you will discover some useful and confidence building techniques, along with practical advice which has assisted in numerous candidates scoring very highly at the assessment centre.

Each of the four exercises are broken down into two components. The Preparation Phase and The Activity Phase (when you actually enter a room and meet the role play actor). All of the information about The Westshire ® Centre is sent to you in advance and you are to use this, along with the brief provided to you in the Preparation Phase, to formulate your plan for the Activity Phase.

Before You Attend The Day
A great deal of people who attended on one of our courses, turned up with their copy of The Westshire ® Centre information pack, much of it with scribbles and notes or huge highlighted sections of information that they believe is relevant.

Here is a huge hint **"Don't try and remember it all"**

Why? Well simply because there is too much information to take in! You will be placed into an unnatural and stressful situation, accessing your memory powers and normal working processes will be greatly hindered by this. So what information should you retain? What is useful and relevant?

In this section of this book, I would really encourage you to do every step of the following process.

Building A Relevant Memory Tool
Do you have a perfect memory? Probably not you will probably be thinking. But, I am sure you can recall significant past events, situations or emotionally charged occurrences from your distant past. Why? How does your brain recall these events with absolute clarity, yet filters out loads of other memories so that they become clouded and vague?

Think of your brain as a super computer, searching through all the files on its hard drive, looking for reference points to an event. The more relevant reference points to a particular folder and file, the easier it is for the computer to locate the information, retrieve it and display it on the screen, your memory.

Let's consider how we all experience the world, it's through our senses of Sight, Sound, Feel, Taste all linked with Emotional Response. Think of these as the data input to your memory file and also reference points when your brain decides to store away the experience. It makes sense then that, the greater the number of reference points, with absolute detail and linked data, the easier it is to retrieve at a later date.

We learn and experience the world through our senses. What is really interesting is that there are variations in people as to which sense or learning/language style we prefer. Some are Visual people, using sight as a predominant learning experience. Some people are Auditory people, where music or sound has a greater influence on them and so on.

I assume, I haven't met you yet, unless you will have been on one of our fantastic one day courses where we have great fun, getting this firmly stuck in your memory, for you to use at the assessment centre. Follow this process and I promise you, having bumped into previous course attendees a year or two later, it will still be accessible from your memory.

First off, let us put the fictitious retail and leisure complex into a familiar context.

In a moment, I would like you to close your eyes and think about your local, regional shopping centre. Somewhere like, Bluewater in Kent or The Oracle in Reading or the Bull Ring in Birmingham. Hopefully you have visited somewhere like this.

Think about walking around the mall areas, the sounds, the lights, the colour of the flooring, how busy it is on a Saturday morning with families and others around.

Close your eyes for just 2 minutes and think about it so that it is crystal clear in your mind.

Done it? Make sure you have before you move on, no cheating here, it won't help you!

Assuming you have let's move on.

That place you remembered and walked around in your minds eye, is from now on called "The Westshire ® Centre". When thinking about the centre, visualise that place to give you mental context of the environment. For the purpose of the Interactive Exercises and Written Exercises, you have to believe you work there, so immerse yourself in that role.

Grab a spare piece of paper and a pen!!

The description of the centre states that it has 2 floors so draw 2 parallel horizontal lines like below on your piece of paper. Spread them out a bit more than this.

These are to remind you that the centre has two floors. Why, because if you enter a role play and don't ask the relevant questions, eg **"where did you last see this gentleman, was he upstairs or downstairs?"** you may miss some important information.

The centre is described as having numerous car parking spaces and disabled parking bays for disabled badge holders, it has good transportation links to many nearby towns and villages etc. There are 156 shops and blah blah. Much of this is irrelevant, because if you visualise your local regional shopping centre, do you know, *"how many car parking spaces there are?"* No! *"Do you know all of its transport links?"* Probably not. *"Do you know how many shops are in the centre?"* No!

Discard all of this as it's not a priority to remember.

Do remember that "Wheelchairs are available for free, from the main customer services desk"

This will form an important part of your memory tool creation.

Back to our memory tool.

"Downstairs in the middle of the centre is the Food Court where there is a Bar". This is important to remember as a bar is where alcoholic beverages are served and alcohol can equal trouble.

Add these two your memory tool.

Food Court
BAR

"Next door to the Food Court is the Main Customer Services Desk." Add this also to your diagram

Food Court	Customer Services Desk
BAR	

"Wheelchairs are available for free from the Main Customer Services Desk". Why is this relevant? Well wheelchairs are normally required by people with some form of Medical condition or ailment. This helps you link the next items together.

"The centre has a Medical Centre, staffed by a Registered Nurse and other qualified first aiders" Knowing this is extremely useful for the role plays if given a scenario which may contain an injured or potentially injured person that needs attention. Add the Medical Centre to your diagram.

Food Court	Customer Services Desk	Medical Centre
BAR		

There are a number of teams that also work in the centre, these can be used as part of the broader role play scenarios, to assist you in your resolutions to potential issues.

Housekeeping – There are a number of housekeepers in the centre who are there to maintain tidiness and cleanliness of the facilities. These people are useful for SPILLS or MESS which represent a safety hazard to you, members of the public or other staff members.

Security Team – At any one time there <u>are 8 -20 security guards on duty</u>, for the protection and health and safety of customers and visitors to the centre. Remember that <u>8 is also the same number of CCTV cameras dotted around the centre.</u> CCTV can be used for all sorts of activities.

Police Officers – 2 Police Officers are present in the centres own Police Station, which is manned only when the centre is open. They are there for any serious problems, such as crimes etc.

Drawn these three teams on your diagram so that it now looks like this.

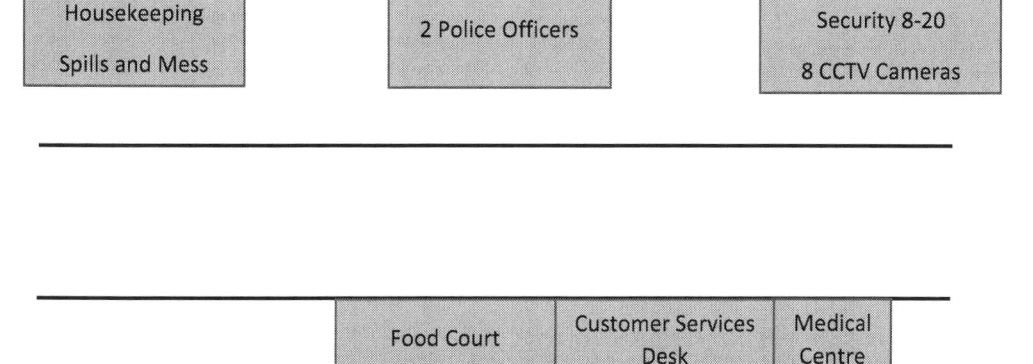

Housekeeping	2 Police Officers	Security 8-20
Spills and Mess		8 CCTV Cameras

Food Court	Customer Services Desk	Medical Centre
BAR		

Your main duties and responsibilities as a Customer Services Officer are all directly linked to the 6 Core Competencies of a Police Officer. This page in the document should be recognised as such and matching the two roles should be easily realised.

Importantly, in your role as a Customer Services Officer, you "do not supervise staff". This scenario setting remember, is directly linked to the role of a Police Constable, not a Sergeant or Inspector with management responsibilities.

Within the information pack sent to you, there is one bullet point of particular importance. It states:

- Making announcements over the tannoy

This innocuous little sentence is actually exceptionally important to you and your success in some of the potential role plays you may face. Using the tannoy is your means of involving other members of the greater team, in assisting you in the given scenario.

There will be no actual "tannoy" system for you to use, instead, consider explaining your thought process and what you would do, to the role play actor.

For example, the role play actor states that there is a situation in the centre whereby an elderly lady was surrounded by a group of youths after she slipped on the wet floor. Whilst she was on the floor it is believed that she was injured and the youths set about taking her purse.

Here is how to utilise the tannoy.

First explain that the lady's injuries are your priority and that the centre has a Medical Centre, staffed by a trained nurse who can administer first aid. After confirming the location of the lady state "I'm just going to use the tannoy to ask the nurse to go to that location to help the lady"

You briefly turn to one side, breaking eye contact with the role play actor and then state "Ok, I've done that now, help is on its way." You can then expand on this by using the rest of the team EG:

"You say that this lady slipped over on the wet floor, that's very concerning as it will also represent a trip hazard to other customers and staff, I will inform the Housekeeping Team to attend and clear that up. Also, this group of youths have allegedly committed a crime so I will contact the two Police Officers and our Security Team, to have them tracked down and investigated appropriately, I will just get those teams in action using the tannoy. Ok, I have done that and they are on their way. Please give me more information on......."

When running our One Day Training Courses, some people would state they are nervous about explaining the use of a tannoy. You are essentially acting and people also feel uncomfortable about this. Please try not to as this skill set is no different to the role of a Police Officer. Consider this, whilst out on patrol as a fully-fledged serving Police Officer, you come across a road traffic collision. A motorcyclist has been killed, along with one occupant of a motor vehicle which is on it's roof. You are the first on scene and the driver of the car is alive and conscious but trapped an in considerable pain. Naturally you will ensure your own safety before approaching the scene etc, but then you would probably attend to this last surviving casualty. I would suggest that the conversation would go along the lines of

"Please try to remain calm, I can see you are in pain and I want to get help here as quickly as possible. I am just going to use my **RADIO** to contact the Fire Brigade and the Ambulance services so that we can get you out and looked after....."

Or words to that effect.

Your tannoy at the One Day Assessment Centre is the equivalent to a serving Police Officer's radio. Don't be afraid to use it! Now add it to your memory picture like so:

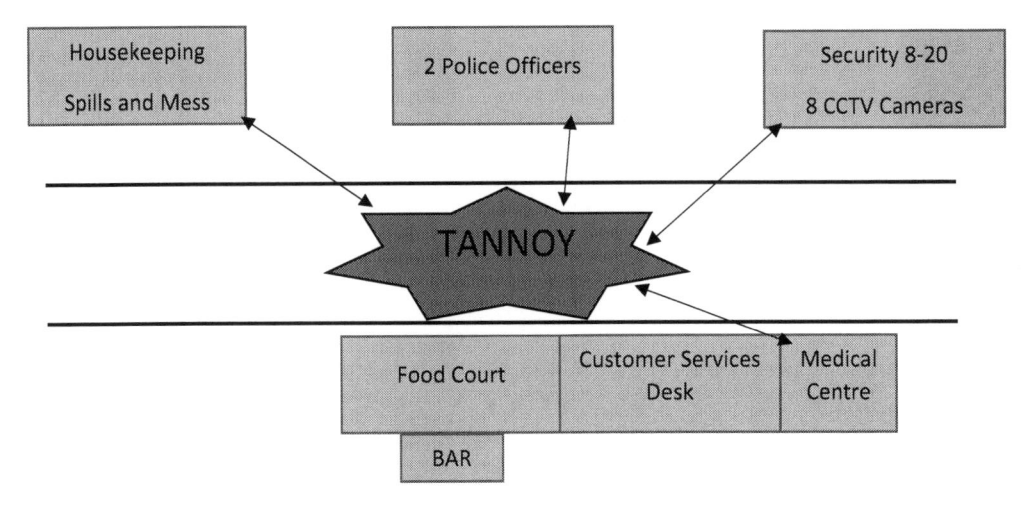

Housekeeping	2 Police Officers	Security 8-20
Spills and Mess		8 CCTV Cameras

TANNOY

Food Court	Customer Services Desk	Medical Centre

BAR

Equality Policy Statement

The centres Equality Policy Statement is a reference to pure respect for race and diversity. Updated in approximately 2014 to keep up with more prominent equality legislation the EPS is there to protect both staff, customers and visitors to the centre. Essentially you must ensure that no one breeches this statement whilst in the role play EG; use offensive or derogatory language about someone's age, sex, sexual orientation, gender reassignment, race, religion or belief, disability, marriage and civil partnership or pregnancy and maternity. This applies to discrimination and or harassment.

Harassment includes any unwanted conduct (including words, behaviour or a combination of both) directed at person on the basis of any of the above mentioned factors, which has the purpose or effect of violating their dignity or creating an intimidating, hostile, degrading, humiliating or offensive environment.

The centre does not tolerate discrimination or harassment of any kind.

It is important for you to have a good understanding of this and the three steps outlined in the complaints procedure for The Westshire ® Centre. These three steps are

A – Ask the other person to stop. This means someone may not be doing something with the intention of discriminating the victim or harassing them. If they are asked to stop what they are doing and they comply, then the matter needs to go no further

B- Talk to an appropriate person about the situation to establish if there is discrimination or harassment. Guess who this person will be? Yes, it will be YOU the Customer Services Officer.

C- Complain in writing to the centres Operations Manager who will investigate the situation and take the appropriate actions.

Add the Equality Policy Statement to your memory picture like so:

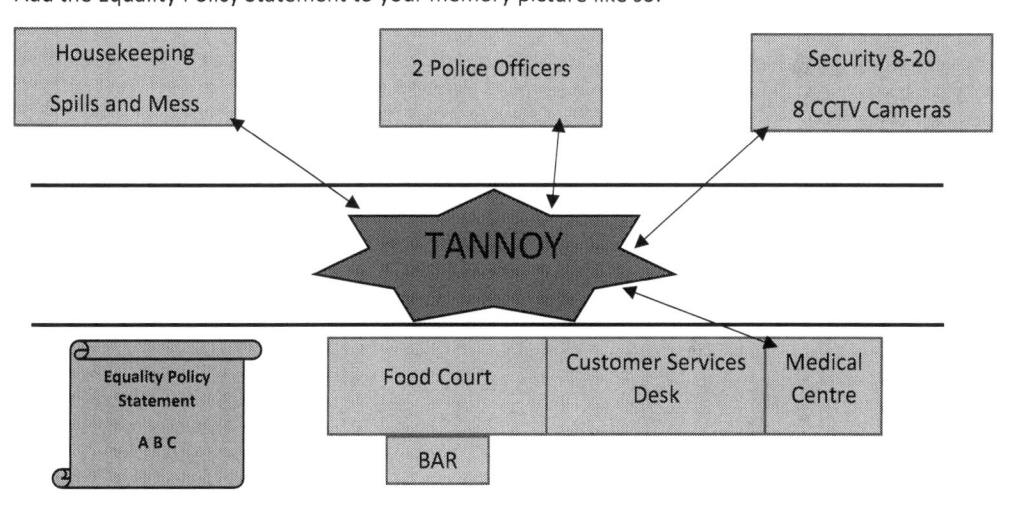

Housekeeping	2 Police Officers	Security 8-20
Spills and Mess		8 CCTV Cameras

TANNOY

Equality Policy Statement A B C	Food Court	Customer Services Desk	Medical Centre
	BAR		

Code of Conduct

The centres Code of Conduct is basically a list of do's and don'ts. Most of these are relatively common sense EG; not misusing escalators, blocking walkways or using offensive language or behaving antisocially. If anyone is found to be not abiding with the code, then the centre reserves the right to escort them away from the premises and ban them if appropriate. Remember, if someone uses foul or offensive language in the role play, you **must** challenge it firmly but appropriately.

Add this to the diagram.

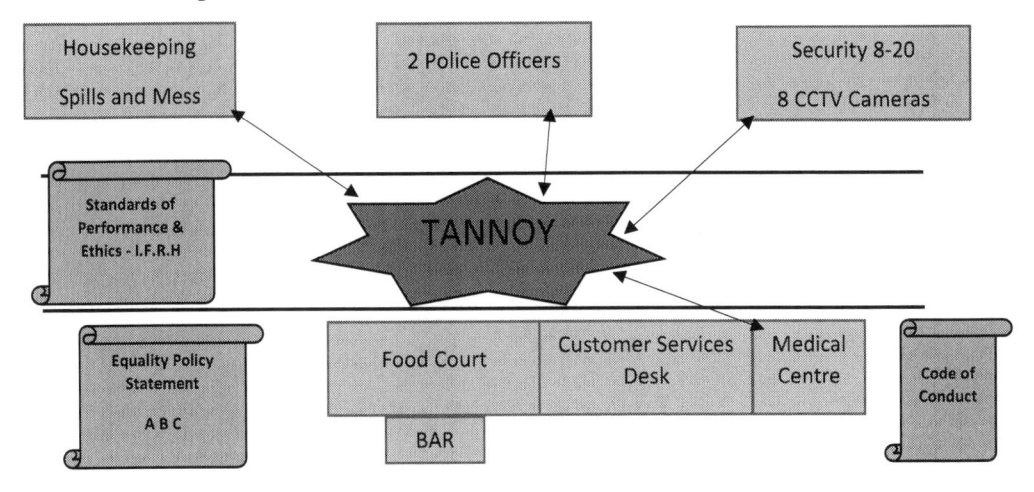

```
Housekeeping              2 Police Officers           Security 8-20
Spills and Mess                                       8 CCTV Cameras

  Standards of
  Performance &              TANNOY
  Ethics - I.F.R.H

                          Food Court   Customer Services   Medical
  Equality Policy                      Desk                Centre       Code of
  Statement                                                             Conduct
  A B C                         BAR
```

IMPORTANT UPDATE - 2017: The police service have now introduced an additional document into the Westshire Centre structure. This is termed Standards of Performance and Ethics. This new set of guidelines will effect your role plays and the future assessment centres – pay particular attention to anything new is my advice!

The Westshire Standards of Performance and Ethics effects all members of the Westshire Centre staff and relates to the following key principles.

Integrity –

- You must always act in the interest of customers.
- You must provide a high level of service.
- You must challenge /report improper language or behaviour from colleagues or customers in an appropriate manner.

Fairness –

- You must treat everyone fairly regardless of age, gender, ethnicity or any other personal characteristic.
- You must not act in ways which are biased or prejudiced for or against others.

Respect –

- You must show respect to both colleagues and customers regardless of the situation.
- You must use language appropriately and sensitively with others.

Honesty –

- You must be honest in your interactions with people.
- You must clarify any ambiguities and not misrepresent any facts when dealing with colleagues or customers.

Now that your memory tool is complete, practice it and learn it. You should ensure you are able to draw all of these elements and link them together. Why is this so important? Well something on this diagram will be able to assist you in 99% of the role plays that the One Day Assessment Centre can through at you.

Try to remember it with the following paragraph.

"The centre has 2 floors, downstairs in the middle is the food court, where there is a bar. Next door to this is the Customer Services Desk, where you can get wheelchairs for free. Wheelchairs reminded me of a medical condition and that the centre also has a Medical Centre, staffed by a nurse. He/She is useful for first aid. There are also a Housekeeping Team, useful for spills and mess, a Security Team, 8 -20 of them and 8 reminds me that there are also 8 CCTV cameras around the centre. There are also 2 Police Officers and I can get hold of all of these people using the TANNOY. The centre operates under an Equality Policy Statement, which has 3 steps, ASK them to stop, Come and see ME and finally to COMPLAIN in writing. Alongside the Equality Policy Statement, there is also a Code of Conduct. I must at all times abide by the Statement of Performance and Ethics – Integrity, Fairness, Respect and Honesty"

Draw the diagram, repeat the words. Draw it again and continue to repeat the process until you have it firmly lodged in your mind. This way, when you attend the assessment centre, as part of your preparation for each role play. You will be able to note this diagram down and use it to your advantage.

Preparation Phase

The first part of each role play is when you are given 5 minutes to prepare and study an information brief. You are allowed to make notes and take these into the role play with you. The briefs are normally quite long but not overly detailed. Try not to fall into the trap of planning how you will handle the situation. That probably seems counter intuitive, to NOT plan. However, it has been proven time and time again that candidates that enter the Activity Phase of the scenario, go into the room, with a structured plan that is almost instantly rendered useless by the brief that the role play actor has been given. My advice to all candidates is "don't plan". Make some key notes and draw the memory tool diagram. Go into the situation like you would today in your day job. For example, very few people who, will be told that there is a complaining customer that needs attention, sit down and "plan" the conversation:

"I will say this and he will probably say that. Then I will do this and he will do that...."

Most people take the initial brief of information, extract key information then go to the customer and say "How can I help?" Then react to the customer appropriately. Too often, when placed in role play scenarios people will think and plan too much. Be natural and confident in your own abilities.

Activity Phase

In the Activity Phase you will enter the room and meet the role play actor, normally they are seated. There will also be an Assessor in the room. Don't worry about this person, remain focused on the role play actor. When you enter the room, have something to say. That is, don't enter the room and be blithering or uncertain how to start the conversation. Try;

"Hi, my name is…………… I am the Customer Services Officer, how can I help you?"

Don't offer your hand for a handshake, it won't be accepted and you will be left standing with your arm outstretched and feeling a little deflated.

Use questions, lots of them! Questions are your friends and a skilled questioner will be able to extract more or hidden information that the role play actor may have been brief to retain unless asked numerous times.

Open questions have who, where, what, why, when or how at the start. These are great for conversation or topic openers.

"Okay, please tell me how this happened?"

"Why do you think this happened?"

Closed questions can clarify a position and have only an alternative answer, A or B.

"Was his shirt a long sleeve (A) or a short sleeve (B) design?"

Try to remember that not all role plays have a solution, it may be that the role play actor's brief is to decline any suggestions you make or to reject any recommendations. You can of course ask them for their suggestions but, you will probably find they will decline to provide any. Select your best course of action and pursue this as the strategy for moving the situation going forwards.

Police Officer role play actors tend to be seated nowadays, and the scenarios are never violent or overly threatening, so relax and expect some low level hostility but nothing that would cause you harm or severe distress. From the feedback I have received from numerous sources, the majority of role plays are based on equality and respect for diversity. This fits in with the Equality Policy Statement and if the role play actor uses offensive or derogatory language, you must challenge it!

To challenge inappropriate or offensive language you should employ a technique I call a "Requested Order". This is not as direct as saying to someone;

"You can't say that" or "Don't say things like that". These could come across as antagonistic or argumentative, in any case too forceful. On the flip side you need to be strong than just saying "Please don't say things like that".

A Requested Order uses tonality of voice and specific language to turn a request into an order. Here is the language;

"Please refrain from using derogatory terms or offensive language. We don't tolerate that here at the Westshire Centre. Please, just stick to the facts. Is that okay?"

Tonality is a little tricky to convey in a book but emphasis and assertiveness need to be translated in the phrasing above for the request to evolve into an order.

""Please *refrain from using derogatory terms or offensive language.* **We don't tolerate that here** at the Westshire Centre. **Please, just stick to the facts**. Is that okay?"

The italics would represent assertiveness, the bold underlined sections more force in your tonality and phrasing.

Role Play Scenarios

In the pre-circulated information provided in the joining instructions for the SEARCH One Day Assessment, you will be furnished very vague and brief explanations about the interactive exercises. The document will tend to provide the last names of the role play actors character, for example;

- Gamer, a shop owner in the centre, wants to discuss an incident that recently happened in the centre.
- Kowalski, a shop owner in the centre who wants to discuss an incident in their shop.
- Swift, a member of the community has asked for a meeting at the centre.
- Zajak, a business owner in the centre, who wants to discuss an incident in their shop.

As you can see these give nothing away in advance of attending. The full briefs at the assessment centre are also still fairly vague but provide a little more substance to the nature of the meeting you are about to enter.

In the past, scenarios have been varied and could include:

- Helping a parent who has lost their child
- Discussing a member of staff's continued lateness
- Discussing a group or particular ethnicity with a shop owner who he/she believes is trouble
- A member of the public complaining about security officers who work at the centre
- A shop owner who is not happy a security officer has not been present or left their post and something happened

Ensure you are using your ears more than your mouth. Sometimes you have to listen very carefully to the role play actor to work out what they ARE saying and more importantly what they are NOT saying! Small comments and vague responses should arouse your curiosity, follow it through and explore every small detail.

Dealing with Complaining People

Below is a technique which is used to provide great customer service, discover why people are complaining and enables the introduction of possible remedies or solutions. If you are faced with a complaint follow this format and you won't go far wrong.

L

Listen to the complainant, genuinely! Use body language like nodding the head and smiling to show you are listening. Say things like "Yes, okay, I understand, go on"

A

Acknowledge their problem. This is where you get to demonstrate empathy and shoehorn in loads of Core Competency type phrases. "I can understand why you are upset by this, I would probably feel the same if I was in your shoes" "Here at the centre, we want to deliver the best customer service possible" "We are a very community based centre and want to ensure everyone feels included..."

P

Probe the problem. This is where you have to start using your questioning skills to establish the root cause of the problem. Most people will complain at a very high level with a broad statement. "Your shopping centre is bloody awful!" You need to drill down into the problem and find out exactly what has caused that perspective. Once you have completed this and you feel you have isolated it, you can move on.

S

Sidestep the root cause. Say something like "Ok, let's put that issue to one side for a second. Are you happy with X, and have you been pleased with Y......" Your tactic here is to get the person to start confirming everything else is okay or good. Once you have got a few yes's move back to the root issue and say "So if I could provide you with a solution to this area (the root cause), everything would be okay?" Now if they say "Yes" congratulations you definitely found your root cause. If however they say "No", circle back around to Probe and start again as you missed something.

10 Top Tips for the Interactive Exercises

1. Use the memory diagram. Draw it on a very small piece of paper that fits in the palm of your hand and take it into every role play. Something on there will help you
2. Don't plan how the conversation will pan out, you will be wrong. Make notes of the pertinent information on the back of your memory diagram. You can always refer to it in the activity phase
3. Have something to say when entering the room. "Hi, my name is............... I am the Customer Services Officer, how may I help you?" Be confident and assertive but not arrogant or threatening
4. Listen carefully to the role play actor, act on what they do and sometimes do not say. If something is unclear, question it
5. Questions are your friends. Use them in abundance
6. Introduce as many keywords and phrases from the Core Competencies are possible to score higher
7. Don't assume you will be able to resolve the problem
8. Use requested orders rather than direct orders
9. Recap information with the role play actor to clarify your understanding of what has been said and their understanding of your proposals
10. Don't be afraid to use the team around you via introducing the Tannoy technique

CHAPTER 9 - THE WRITTEN TESTS

New Style Tests Introduced in September 2015

The College of Policing recently released new pre assessment day materials for all candidates. In particular the written test section of the one day assessment has significantly changed.

Regardless of whether the written tests are completed before or during the assessment centre, all candidates will complete two written exercises. Both exercises will last for circa 30 minutes. You will be shown into an exercise room along with the other candidates in your group. You will also receive a thorough briefing before you start each exercise. Paper and pens are provided, together with documents to write your response. You may make rough notes on a separate piece of paper, which will not be assessed.

The written skills being tested at the assessment centre are your ability to comprehend and summarise information accurately, structure responses logically and to use spelling and grammar correctly.

Here are the two new exercise descriptions:

Written exercise one – you will be asked to read typed instructions before using this information to complete an incident report form.

Written exercise two – you will be asked to make notes while watching a DVD of a person being interviewed about an incident that they have witnessed. You will then use these notes to complete an incident report form.

Top 10 Tips for Completing Successful Responses

1. Write in full sentences, not bullet points or notes
2. Structure your responses in a logical fashion, each must have a beginning, middle and an end
3. Do not use jargon or slang terms, this is a formal test for a very important occupation
4. Ensure your spelling and punctuation are as perfect as possible
5. Incorporate as many key words and phrases as possible from the Core Competency document
6. If asked to make suggestions ensure they are logical and within the boundaries of the brief provided. EG; do not add any outside information
7. Listen very carefully to the DVD and make note of the pertinent information
8. Do not assume anyone is guilty of an offense or crime unless all facts are known
9. Structure your time accordingly, the beginning of the response should not take too long to complete, the middle the greater amount of time as this is where your main findings and keywords will appear. The end should also be rather brief.
10. Double check your document before finally submitting it on the day.

This guide is based on the teachings in our new online course that is available at

www.moneytreemasters.co.uk

Don't waste £'s or your valuable time attending an <u>expensive one day course</u>.

Sit back, relax and gain expert information, at your own pace and with the ability to review and recap all elements of the course 24/7

CHAPTER 10 – Verbal Logical Reasoning Tests

The Verbal Logical Reasoning test measures your ability to make sense of a situation when you are given specific written information about it. The test is split into two sections – Section A and Section B. Section A of this test has **three** possible answers where only ONE of which is correct, whereas Section B has **four** possible answers of which only ONE is correct.

In **Section A** they will give you a number of conclusions which you might come to. You must look at each conclusion and work out if:

A the conclusion is **true** given the situation described and the facts known about it;

B the conclusion is **false** given the situation described and the facts known about it; or

C it is **impossible to say** whether the conclusion is true or false given the situation described and the facts known about it.

In **Section B** they will give you four statements and you will be required to evaluate which ONE of the **four** statements is the best answer, given the information provided.

Once you have made your decision you will then fill in the appropriate space on an answer sheet provided.

The real test is has 28 questions and is 30 minutes long.

Here is an example question.

At 10.30 this morning Constable Shan collected the CCTV footage from the Bessies Corner Shop on High Street. She started to review the CCTV footage of an incident at 14.30 on the previous afternoon.

While watching the footage she observed two women, wearing hooded tops (one pink and one blue), enter the shop through the door at the side. The time recorded on the footage was 13.45. The women stood at the back of the shop, with only their backs in the view of the CCTV camera.

There were five other people in the shop, three customers and a male sales assistant, at the time. The customers were a man, two women and a child. At 14.05 the one female, the child and the man, who appeared to be together, left the shop after paying for several items including tea and pasta.

The other customer paid for a bottle of orange juice and left the shop at 14.21. At 14.22 the woman in the pink hooded top approached the sales assistant, who was behind the counter at the front of the shop, and appeared to speak to him.

At this time the other woman was standing near the entrance of the shop. After the exchange with the shop assistant the woman took what appeared to be a large knife from her pocket and waved this in front of the sales assistant. The sales assistant appeared to open the till and then the woman seemed to pass a hold-all over the counter.

At 14.40 the sales assistant started filling the bag. Constable Shan then observed the shop door open and what appeared to be a woman entering the shop. The woman who had been standing at the back of the shop stepped forward and punched the woman who had been entering the shop. The woman who had thrown the punch then shouted at her friend, who then grabbed the holdall from the sales assistance before running out of the shop.

Select one of the below options for each of the questions below:

A = TRUE					B = FALSE					C = IMPOSSIBLE TO SAY

1.	At 10.00 this morning Constable Shan knew there were two women involved in the robbery.
2.	The woman who punched the customer spoke to the sales assistant.
3.	At 14.05 there were more men in the shop than women.
4.	The customer who bought the orange juice will be able to provide a description of the two women.

Answers

1. Impossible to say
2. False
3. False
4. Impossible to say

CHAPTER 11 – Numerical Reasoning Tests

The new numerical tests are now calculator based tests rather than mental arithmetic.

What will happen during the numerical ability test?

In the numerical ability test you will be asked to answer multiple choice questions which will measure your ability to use numbers in a rational way, correctly identifying logical relationships between numbers and drawing conclusions and inference from them. Please note that the test will not assess simple numerical checking ability.

You will be presented with a series of graphs and tables, each followed by several questions. You must choose the correct answer from a maximum of four possible answers, filling in the appropriate space on an answer sheet provided at the assessment centre. The questions will require you to utilise the following numerical operations:

- Addition
- Subtraction
- Multiplication
- Division
- Averages (mean)
- Percentages
- Ratios
- Interpretation of numbers represented graphically

You will take the test in an exercise room along with the other candidates in your group. You can use a calculator for this test which will be provided for you by the assessment centre assessors. You are not permitted to use your own calculator during this test. Before the start of the test the assessors will give you full instructions.

The numerical ability test will last for 23 minutes and there are 21 questions in the test.

Here is an example question:

The local constabulary has put out to tender for the supply of vehicle maintenance services to a number of vehicle repair and servicing specialists. Below are quotes from 3 specialists. The quotes cover differing periods of time.

	Supplier 1 (1yr)	Supplier 2 (3yrs)	Supplier 3 (5yrs)
Routine Vehicle Services	£21,450	£64,520	£119,120
Annual Road Safety and Legal Checks	£11,550	£35,122	£54,150
Incidental Repairs and Accidental damage	£15,654	£48,150	£79,120

1. What percentage of the total quotation from Supplier 1 does Routine Vehicle Services account for?
   a. 42%
   b. 47%
   c. 40%
   d. 44%
2. Based on an annual one year cost, which supplier provides the cheapest quote for Annual Road Safety and Legal Checks?
   a. Supplier 1
   b. Supplier 2
   c. Supplier 3
   d. They are the same
3. Based on an annual one year cost, which supplier provides the most expensive quote for Incidental Repairs and Accidental Damage?
   a. Supplier 2
   b. Supplier 1
   c. Supplier 3
   d. They are the same

Answers

1. 44%
2. Supplier 3
3. Supplier 2

Please join the online course and download these additional free materials as they are updated.

Top Ten Tips for Passing the Psychometric Tests

1. Practice, practice and practice some more. Most candidates will not have used mathematical skills or be used to the style of questioning used in the Verbal Logical Reasoning test.
2. Begin your practice with just a few examples every day. Do not use timed exercises in the first instance. Concentrate on accuracy.
3. With the Numerical Tests, focus on the "method" rather than the outcome. You will have a calculator to provide the outcome/result. You need to know how to get there.
4. Two weeks ahead of the assessment centre, change your practice regime and begin using timed exercises, this will begin to increase your speed of working.
5. If you get stuck, move on and come back to the question at the end, don't waste time
6. Listen carefully to the assessors instructions
7. Remember these tests are carried out in exam conditions. Failure to observe these rules will mean you are excluded from the tests and subsequently fail the assessment day.
8. The exam papers use a tick box style answer sheet, mark clearly your final answers on this document and this is what will used to score your performance
9. Relax during the test. Stress causes you to lose concentration
10. Work quickly and accurately, if you don't know the answer, guess and move on

CHAPTER 12 – One Day Assessment Interview

Much has changed about the SEARCH ® One Day Assessment Interview recently. Previously the College of Policing would provide you with 4 questions, each based on a particular Core Competency and you could therefore prepare very fully in advance.

The new interview guidance provided to us and through our sources suggests that the new interview is radically different, yet surprisingly similar. The major change is that all 6 Core Competencies are assessed throughout and there are only two clearly defined "Competency" based questions.

NB from the Author "Refer back Chapter 5 for techniques on how to tackle Competency and Motivational questions"

There are also two further questions which will relate to what is described as, "your motivations and values".

This will mean that there will need to be additional research and a succinct response to ensure your success at passing this interview.

The One Day Assessment Interview is unlike any other "normal" job interview you will attend. Conditions are set out to be very sterile and the experience can fell quite "cold". This means that you will gain very little feedback from the interviewer.

The Police service set up the interview in this way to ensure absolute fairness for all candidates who attend the assessment centre. They do not want more emotive or emotional things to effect the judgement of the assessor. For example, you would normally enter an interview, be greeted, shake hands and small talk about your journey and some other things before starting the "formal" interview. At the One Day Assessment Centre, this is not the same.

You will enter a room, there will be the interviewer sat down and they will offer you a chair. Do not shake hands, they won't accept the offer and you will feel a little daft and start losing confidence. They will not engage in any small talk and will begin by asking you the first question. They will also hand you a piece of paper or a booklet which has the same question written down for your reference. You are then expected to talk for 5 minutes about that question.

During this interview the assessor may not even look at you, instead focusing on their marking sheet, scribbling away and avoiding eye contact etc.

Why so sterile?

Well as mentioned, the Police service want to avoid emotive and emotional judgement calls on you and all candidates. This is to ensure there is no chance of prejudice or bias on their part. They want to base the decisions purely on the information you provide and your ability to communicate effectively.

There are numerous studies that show that those who practice and use techniques to improve their "likeability" will be 55% more successful in securing a position. But this is not based on fact or fairness, this is based on human interaction. Unfortunately this is something that can also then be construed as prejudice or discriminatory. As such, the One Day Assessment interview is very closed and sterile.

That said our recommended approach is to still try to influence these matters. Your goal for any interview in the Police selection process is quite simple.

Get them to like you and show you have the right qualities.

Questions Types in the Interview

There are two types, Motivational and Competency. In Chapter 5, we went into great detail on how to approach these differing styles of questions. As a short reminder.

Competency Questions x2

Here you must prepare your responses in advance of attending the interview. This way, when you are asked the question you will be able to commit and engage quickly and in a structured way. This will demonstrate confidence and effective communication.

To prepare in advance consider each of the Core Competencies and write out 2 scenarios where you have demonstrated key elements for each of them. Write them out using the STAR technique mentioned in Chapter 5.

How much preparation should I do?

Script writers use the following equation:

45 minutes of writing will roughly equate to 5 minutes worth of speaking.

That means you will need to complete.

12 x 45 minutes of writing STAR examples (2 for each Core Competency) You need two as 1 will be a back-up scenario in case you forget the first. These will be your first draft.

Second Draft – Go back over each of your examples, and check them against the Core Competencies mentioned earlier in this study guide. Ensure you have matched the competency and included lots of keywords and phrases. These are the words the interviewer will be looking out for so make sure they are clear and evident when you talk about them. This will take about an additional 20 minutes per scenario.

12x45 = 540 minutes

12x20 = 240 minutes

540 + 240 = 780 minutes = 13 hours preparation for 2 potential questions. Sounds a lot right?!

The better prepared you are, the more successful you will be. Once you have your finished scenarios, keep reminding yourself of them but don't try to learn them word for word. You will be under pressure on the day, so learning "lines" is not the right approach. Learn the structure.

S

T

A

R

As you will be using real events you have experienced (don't lie) your brain will be able to recall and enable you to recite those key elements.

Motivations and Values x2

These questions are a new format for the One Day Assessment Centre.

There are three major concerns any organisation has when recruiting new people.

1. Are you the right person for the job? EG Do you have the right skills and do you know what the job is all about?
2. Are you going to fit in culturally?
3. Are we going to get a return on our recruitment and training investment

Point 1 is assessed by the Competency based questions whereas, 2 and 3 are more in tune with your motivations and values.

To prepare for these questions you will need complete a great deal of research on the constabulary you wish to join and apply the techniques mentioned in Chapter 5.

You will recall we mentioned the headline question of

"Why do you want to become a Police Officer?"

You can utilise the same techniques here to overcome these questions with ease.

Here is the structure broken down into sections:

Section 1 – Employer Organisation Understanding and Values Alignment
Section 2 – Understanding the Role and Evidence of Skill Set
Section 3 – Flippancy and Concentration Recovery
Section 4 – Close the Conversation

The assessors may ask you open questions to test your values Eg:

"What are your opinions on immigration?"
"What type of people commit crimes?"
"What is your view on legalising cannabis use?"

These "Value" questions can be a little daunting. The key to answering these is to approach them in exact accordance with the Core Competencies. Ask yourself, "What would a model police officer say to that question?"

You will need to ensure that you are balanced and fair in your responses. Do not say something that could cause rise to a concern in your values or potential prejudices.

Added to the 13 hours of preparation you need to complete for the competency based questions, you will also need to have a full understanding of the values and visions of the constabulary you wish to join. If in total you are doing less than 16 hours preparation for this 20 minute interview. You are probably doing yourself a disservice.

CHAPTER 13 – Interviews

(Telephone, One Day and Final Interviews)

Interview preparation needs to be broken down into 3 major areas

You

Research

Questions

This is regardless of whether the interview is over the telephone, at the assessment centre or any potential final interview.

You

The most fundament part of preparation is recognising the effect you have on the interview process. Remember that over 60% of all hiring decisions are based on one factor alone "does the interviewer like you?" Challenging, when the Police service don't want this to affect their assessors. However, they are just human beings after all, so we recommend you approach this and use it to your advantage.

- Appearance – Despite anything you may have heard, wear a suit to all interviews and the One Day Assessment Centre. This is a formal uniformed job, so turn up looking the part. Dark coloured suits, black, navy blue are preferred, couple this with a white shirt or blouse for the ladies. Gentlemen should always where a dark coloured plain tie. No mickey mouse or transformers characters on display. (I've seen it done!!?) Fresh haircuts, shiny shoes and if you have facial hair ensure this is neatly trimmed. Ladies should wear their hair tied up in a bun at the back of the head.
- First Impressions Count – depending on which book you read you will have anywhere between 8 and 12 seconds to make a first impression in an interview. This is crucial as ultimately it sets the tone for the rest of the interview. In the first 8 – 12 seconds, how much will you say? Not a huge amount but you are communicating the whole time.

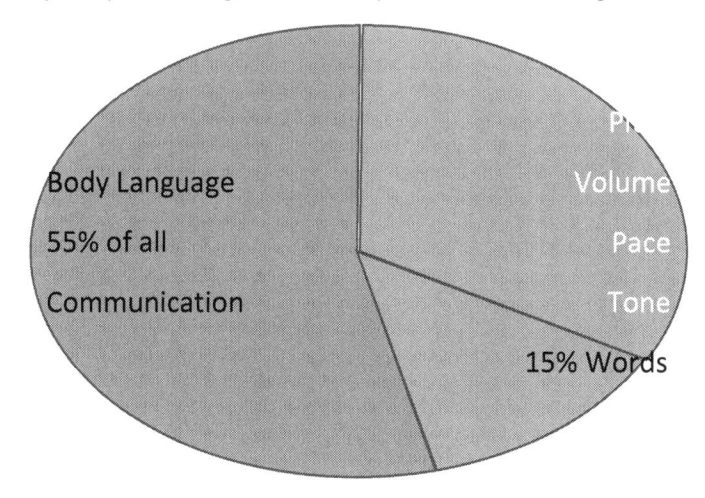

Body Language 55% of all Communication

Volume
Pace
Tone
15% Words

- For a face to face interview the above graph applies. However, for a telephone interview Body Language becomes redundant and effectively is replaced by greater percentages for pitch, volume, pace and tone. This is not what you say, but how you say it. Words, EG the actual language you use is also incredibly important, so ensure you use lots of keywords and phrases from the core competencies. For telephone interviews, make absolutely certain you are in a space where you won't be distracted or disturbed, available at the time of the planned call and have had time to prepare. Take the call standing up, rather than slouched in a chair. This may seem strange, but SMILE as you talk and project your voice a little. The interviewer will be noting down your responses so pace yourself and give them enough time to absorb your words.
- Building rapport with an interviewer quickly in a face to face environment is essential. When you enter the room make eye contact and SMILE. The smile is the quickest way for you to build rapport with another person. You will have heard the phrase "Smile and the whole world smiles with you" I'm sure. This is ultimately true.
- Posture – Consider how you sit in the interview. Ensure you are sitting upright and comfortably. Don't slouch or fold your arms. You need an attentive open posture with your head slightly raised, arms unfolded, knees together but not bolt upright as you would imagine a soldier to sit in a court martial.
- Eye Contact – Try not to lazer beam the back of an interviewer's skull out during an interview. Eye contact is important, when you first enter the room, at the start of the response to a question and when you wish to make a point. But otherwise, look "about" the interviewers face and not directly into their eyes. It becomes rather awkward and unnerving for an interviewer if a candidate is glaring at them throughout.
- Dealing with nerves – If you find yourself becoming over nervous, pause. There is nothing wrong with taking a subtle large breath, composing yourself and then continuing. Recognise that interview nerves come from only one place, YOU. Unfortunately, the only reason you are feeling nervous is because you are having a mental battle with your conscious and sub conscious. Your brain is probably telling you "You are going to mess this up" or "You are going to forget all your answers" or maybe even "The interviewer doesn't like you" Deal with this by having an internal process to go through. (Don't do this out loud in an interview, it may appear rather bizarre) ;-)
    1. Recognise the internal dialect that is occurring and ask yourself "What are you doing?"
    2. Put everything into context by asking yourself "What is the worst that could happen" – By this I mean what is the utmost worst scenario. Not that you don't get the job, not that you might vomit halfway through the interview. The worst thing!
    3. Ask yourself "Is that going to happen" The answer will be "No"
    4. Finally ask yourself "Then why are you doing this to yourself?"

    This technique is used by many people to overcome interviews, presenting to large audiences etc. By following this process, you will automatically reduce your heart rate, calm your nerves and realise that the interview is just a conversation, like thousands of others you have on a weekly basis and that you have nothing to worry about.
- Final Impressions – At the end of an interview, if you are given the opportunity to add anything further, don't waste it. A great deal of candidates fail to use this opportunity to cement their motivation and suitability firmly in the interviewers mind. Think about structuring something like:

> "Firstly thank you for interviewing me. This opportunity means a great deal to me and like I have said, I have completed lots of research in regards to the role of a Police Officer. If you do select me to go further forwards, then I can guarantee that I will go on to become a competent, safe and successful Police Officer. Thank you for your time."

Now using tonality and a little subliminal messaging, you can emphasis certain words and phrases so they stick in the interviewer's mind.

> "Firstly thank you for interviewing me. This opportunity **means a great deal to me** and like I have said, I have completed lots of research in regards to the role of a **Police Officer**. If you do **select me** to go further forwards, then **I can guarantee** that I will go on to **become a competent, safe and successful Police Officer**. Thank you for your time."

If you are going to give an interviewer the eye ball, this is the time to do it. Deliver it with conviction and to belief in yourself.

Research

First segment of research you must complete ahead of attending any interview is to research the role of a Police Constable. By this I mean, you must have a full and complete understanding of the Core Competencies, the day to day activities of a Police Constable and how your skills and abilities relate to those competencies. You will have completed a great deal of research earlier in the process. Go back, recap, revise and remind yourself of this information.

Secondly you need to research the constabulary you wish to join. Gain a thorough understanding of the county/counties they operate in, the local demographics, review and understand their website, in particular their ABOUT US page. On this page there will be key information in regards to the culture and ethos that constabulary are trying to foster in their organisation.

- Visit their website
- Focus on the About Us page and their recruitment sections
- Understand crime figures in the region
- Learn about the demographics of the area/regions in the county. How culturally diverse is it, what communities are represented.
- Understand unique challenges the constabulary face in terms of policing, maybe things like the Channel Tunnel, large football clubs, ports etc.
- Look for any initiatives that they have running, reports and positive statistics they are talking about, these are all useful discussion points in final interviews.

Questions

This is more about having the wit and perception about you to pre-empt the questions you will face in the interview. Do refer back to Chapter 5 for the major question types you will face. Ahead of any interview you attend, consider your responses to these question types and prepare thoroughly for them. This way, when the question comes in the interview, probably not phrased in the exact same manner but very similar, you have an immediate response that you are comfortable and expert in answering with. This ability sets you apart from the standard, reactionary candidates that come ill prepared or uncertain as to how to handle the questions.

You will face

- Warm Up Questions – Throw away questions used to ease you into the interview ie "How was your journey here today?" Remember that you want to demonstrate being motivated and possessing the Core Competencies. Don't respond with just "Fine thanks" which is what most people would come back with. Try, "It was absolutely fine thank you for asking, this opportunity means a great deal to me. I took the opportunity to come down here last week, so that I could plan my journey and find where to park etc. There was no way I was going to be held up for this". Demonstrates motivation, Decision Making and Service Delivery right?
- Motivational Questions – "Why do you want to become a Police Officer?" and "Why do you want to join this particular constabulary?" Refer to Chapter 5 for the complete technique
- Competency Based Questions – Use that STAR technique mentioned in Chapter 5 to overcome these predictable question styles.

Try to remember that even if something goes wrong in an interview, you can use it to your advantage.

Author's short recollection of his Final Interview:

During my recruitment to Kent County Constabulary, my final interview was rather daunting. Having completed the rest of the final recruitment process, only the interview, medical and a home visit was left. I was requested to attend Kent Police HQ in Maidstone and report at the main reception for the final interview. Naturally the day started the night before really, I hadn't slept too well. Nerves had kept me up most of the night, but I was wide awake and full of coffee by the time I arrived at the HQ reception.

Upon arrival and slightly perspiring with ever more nerves, I signed in and bumped into a number of other candidates I had grown to know over the past 8 months of the selection process. Congratulations of reaching this point were quickly shared before everyone then settled into an unease silence. A civilian support staff then escorted us to an awaiting mini bus which then transported us into the grounds of HQ. We arrived at an old detached police house, one of several in the old grounds on HQ. We were then divided into two team of approximately 8.

"Team 1, you will be called individually into room 1. There you will be interviewed before being sent back downstairs to this waiting room. You are not permitted to discuss the questions you face or the content of the interview. After 15 minutes or so, you will be recalled before the interview panel and they will tell you if you have been successful or not. If you have, you will be transported to meet the force doctor for your medical. If you are unsuccessful, you will be transported to the front gates and will not be able to apply for another role with the police for a further 6 months. Good Luck"

We were all then allocated numbers for interview order, I was number four. It now became even more real and my hear rate began to soar. We all sat in silence, twitching and glancing around at each other.

"Number 1, you are up"

The first candidate rose and left the room to a chorus of "Good luck" and "Hope it goes well". We settled down for what seemed like an eternity. I honestly can't recall who else was there that day but when the first person came back down the look on his face was like he'd seen a ghost. He was a little green around the edges to. He sat in silence, occasionally shaking his head.

"Okay Number 1, you can go back up" the civilian support staff announced.

More well wishes then awkward silence as we awaited his return.

Not long after his footsteps rattled through the waiting room as he descended the stairs. As he entered the room, his eyes were alight and a huge beaming smile was stretched across his face.

"I got in, I don't believe it!"

Rowdy congratulations ensued and handshakes all round. It was great to see it go well.

Number 2 followed the same story.

Number 3 was somewhat different. This candidate came down in tears. He didn't make it and the whole mood in the room changed. Everyone was deflated and I comforted the guy and genuinely felt awful for him.

"Right Number 4 please" Oh crap, that's me I thought.

With my heart feeling like it would burst through my chest, like that alien in the famous film, I started ascending the stairs to Room 1. At the top of the stairs I took a huge intake of air, trying to slow myself down and focus on what was about to happen. I reached forwards and knocked on the door.

"Come in" sounded from what seemed an overly deep voice male, stood somewhere between me and the gates of hell.

I entered the room and was instantly surprised to find a very formal interview setting. So formal in fact the panel of 4 were some 15 feet from my chair, on a raised platform, about a meter above me. All rather unnerving and intimidating.

I cleared my throat and squeaked out "Good morning" as I stood next to the chair.

"Please have a seat" said the Chief Inspector, sat third from the left.

The interview progressed and I eased into it, calling on past experience and some of the techniques described in this guide. I'd like to say it was easy, it wasn't but then, I didn't know half as much about interviews, questions, body language as I do now.

Anyway the 15 minutes waiting was awful, I wasn't sure how I'd done and went through the entire range of emotions sat there.

"Okay Number 4, you can go back up" Instantly my heart sank.

Climbing those stairs again was like climbing Everest, covered in treacle. My legs just didn't want to work. Even knocking the door when I got there was a physical effort.

I entered the room and the panel was giving nothing away. No smiles, no frowns, just blank expressions.

"We have a few more questions if that's okay?" asked the Sergeant.

"Of course" I responded, instantly thinking it's all over.

They probed me on a few matters, about my time as a Special Constable and some other items and then the Chief Inspector said. "Well Christopher, congratulations, we'd like to welcome you to Kent Police."

I was instantly elated, relieved and a little dumbstruck, but it was and remains one of the proudest moments of my working life. We discussed some niceties and formal processes and the interview began to draw to a close. The Chief Inspector began rounding things up.

"So, from here you are going to go and have your medical with the force doctor and we look forward to you joining us in the next few months."

"Thank you Sir" I responded eagerly.

"Just one thing" he paused.

"Yes Sir" I asked inquisitively.

"Yes, it's just something myself and the panel felt we should tell you about." He exclaimed

"Sir?" I was completely bemused now.

"Yes, well look, throughout your career in the Police, or whatever you go on to do, you will have to go to other interviews, like your Sergeants or Inspectors interviews" A smile was drawing across his face and his colleague to the left of him started jittering with a suppressed giggle.

"Well the thing is, next time you go for an interview….. Can you get a new suit or get that hole in your crotch sown up?" The panel erupted in laughter and red faced, I checked to see I had actually ripped a hole, exposing my underwear, right in the crotch of my trousers.

"Er.. yes Sir, of course".

I left the room, knowing it was all in good jest and banter. More importantly I knew those officers would never forget me and despite that complete mess up, I still held my own in the interview and passed.

You see, no matter what happens, you probably won't have a nightmare like that in your interview and I still managed to get in!

CHAPTER 14 – Fitness Test

The Police fitness test has changed over the years. It has been somewhat scaled back to meet with the changing role of a front line Police Officer.

The test is now a multistage fitness test, more commonly known as the Bleep Test.

This test involves running to & fro along a 15 metre track, to a series of audible bleeps. The bleeps, during the course of the test get progressively faster. You will need to have reached each side of the track before the next bleep sounds.

Pass: Run to level 5.4 (Approximately 3 1/2 minute)

At the assessment, you will complete the exercise twice. Once as a warm up and once as your official test.

In order to prepare for the physical test, you should practice the test using a downloadable audio from the web.

If you are relatively fit you should be able to reach the required level. Please do not allow yourself to fail this assessment! Fitness tests are clearly defined for candidates and you will have plenty of time to prepare. Unless you are injured on the day, there should be no excuses for failing this part of the selection process.

Level 5.4 is not a hugely taxing level to achieve for most candidates. However, ensure you eat correctly on the night before the assessment, hydrate yourself and stretch out before you commence.

Maintaining a reasonable level of physical fitness is an important part of your own personal safety and that of your colleagues around you during your time as a Police Officer. You will have short foot chases, scuffles and prolonged public order events to manage and potentially contain. These will tire you out, especially with all the kit you will be carrying.

Try to practice this test at least 3 times per week in the 4 weeks ahead of your scheduled physical test date. You will find that if you can achieve this, on the day it will be a breeze.

CHAPTER 15 – Final Thoughts

I hope you have found this guide useful and informative. Once again I would like to stress that information is not the key to success. Yes it helps, but having tactics and a strategy you can use, repeat and model success upon, is far more important.

We used to offer one day training courses for people who were serious about becoming Police Officers but stopped this practice as it was only focused on one geographical area and was becomingly increasingly expensive for candidates. This prevented a number of candidates from attending and benefiting from our knowledge and experience.

Our unique online course offers unrivalled access to all our materials, delivered by our lead tutor and included additional hints and tips. Once you subscribe to the course, all of the materials are available to you 24/7, 365 days a year, **for life**. Most importantly, you don't have to travel, pay for a hotel or the large cost of attending a one day course. We also don't charge and ongoing fee! It's just a single payment which I'm sure you will agree represents excellent value for money.

One high quality course, at a very good single price. Please do take a look and gain further information and tactics from our lead tutor and founder.

Be safe and good luck in your career.

CJ Benham

Founder of PasstheProcess and MoneyTreeMasters.

Please don't forget to leave your feedback on Amazon.

ONLINE COURSE AVAILABLE

Don't waste £'s or your valuable time attending an <u>expensive one day course</u>.

Sit back, relax and gain expert information, at your own pace and with the ability to review and recap all elements of the course 24/7

www.moneytreemasters.co.uk

Printed in Great Britain
by Amazon

40592463R00036